THE BOOKS OF SCRIPTURE

A concise guide to understanding and applying the Bible

Jonathan Sole

Copyright © 2024 Jonathan Sole

"Scripture quotations are from the ESV® Bible (The Holy Bible, English Standard Version®), © 2001 by Crossway, a publishing ministry of Good News Publishers. Used by permission. All rights reserved. The ESV text may not be quoted in any publication made available to the public by a Creative Commons license. The ESV may not be translated in whole or in part into any other language."

*To my wife, Katelyn, for her endless support,
and to my children, Marlee, Harry, Oliver,
Hazel, Natalie, and the twins.*

CONTENTS

Title Page
Copyright
Dedication
Introduction
The Old Testament — 1
THE LAW — 3
Genesis — 4
Exodus — 6
Leviticus — 8
Numbers — 10
Deuteronomy — 12
The Prophets — 15
Joshua — 16
Judges — 18
1&2 Samuel — 20
1&2 Kings — 22
Jeremiah — 24
Ezekiel — 26
Isaiah — 28
Hosea — 30
Joel — 32
Amos — 34
Obadiah — 36

Jonah	38
Micah	40
Nahum	42
Habakkuk	44
Zephaniah	46
Haggai	48
Zechariah	50
Malachi	52
The Writings	55
Ruth	56
Psalms	58
Job	60
Proverbs	62
Ecclesiastes	64
Song of Songs	66
Lamentations	68
Daniel	70
Esther	72
Ezra	74
Nehemiah	76
1&2 Chronicles	78
The New Testament	80
The Gospels and Acts	81
Matthew	82
Mark	84
Luke	86

John	88
Acts	90
The Letters of Paul	93
Romans	94
1 Corinthians	96
2 Corinthians	98
Galatians	100
Ephesians	102
Philippians	104
Colossians	106
1 Thessalonians	108
2 Thessalonians	110
1 Timothy	112
2 Timothy	114
Titus	116
Philemon	118
The General Letters	121
Hebrews	122
James	124
1 Peter	126
2 Peter	128
1 John	130
2 John	132
3 John	134
Jude	136
Revelation	138

Conclusion 140

INTRODUCTION

Have you ever endeavored to read through the Bible only to get discouraged at specific points because you did not understand what you were reading? I know I can relate; I've been there, you have been there, we all have been there at some point or another. Or maybe you have wondered how all these books go together; how does Habakkuk relate to Genesis or Romans? I am sure many other questions of this nature arise among Christians seeking to be faithful in the discipline of Bible intake. Often, we take the approach of reading the Scriptures because we know we should, even when we do not know much of what we are reading. If you can relate to any of these thoughts or feelings, I hope you find this little book a helpful resource for understanding the big picture of the Bible through the individual books.

This book comes from three primary areas: love for the Word of God, Jesus, and his church. I have found all three of these areas to be interrelated in my life. Love for Jesus increases a passion for his Word and a desire to see his church healthy and growing. I have written with the church member in mind to provide an accessible, practical, and applicable overview and summary of the books of Scripture. The goal is to strengthen your grasp of Scripture so that in understanding it better, you will love it more. It is hard to love what we do not know.

The structure that follows is straightforward. Each of the 66 books of Scripture gets an overview, summary, and application. I have carefully selected four key passages from each book that seek to convey the book's theme, summary, or application. A lot was left out when choosing only four passages. I also approach the Bible with the conviction that all Scripture points to Jesus. I have sought to demonstrate the Christ connection in every book of the Bible carefully.

My desire is for you, the reader, to be blessed and grow in the grace and knowledge of the Lord Jesus Christ. May this book equip you and perhaps even spark a fire in you to dive deeper into the word of God. God's word is a treasure by which we can never mine the depths. May Jesus Christ be glorified and the church strengthened until he comes again.

"You search the Scriptures because you think that in them you have eternal life; and it is they that bear witness about me" John 5:39

THE OLD TESTAMENT

The Old Testament (OT) authors wrote over roughly a thousand years. Moses wrote in the 15th century B.C., and Malachi wrote in the late 5th century B.C. However, the story begins with God creating the universe, so the timeline of the OT spans from creation to the year 400 B.C. The OT makes up seventy-five percent of the Bible and is foundational to understanding the New Testament.

Most English Bibles today consider the OT to have 39 books. Some larger narratives split in two during the Hebrew text's translation into Greek due to scroll sizes. Furthermore, the minor prophets are all recognized as individual books instead of the Book of the Twelve, as referred to in the Hebrew Scriptures. The Hebrew Scriptures recognize the same books but break them into 25 instead of 39. Samuel, Kings, Chronicles, The Twelve, and Ezra-Nehemiah have historically been considered single books.

The order of the books in the following pages breaks with the English tradition of law, history, poetry, and prophets (major and minor). Instead, it reflects the structure that Jesus and all the New Testament (NT) authors knew; law, prophets, and writings. The idea is that the one unified story of redemption would emerge by reading the OT the way Jesus did, and the bridge from Chronicles to Matthew would be apparent. The ultimate message is that the loving Creator sends a Rescuer to save his people for his glory and

JONATHAN SOLE

their good.

THE LAW

GENESIS

Author:
Moses is the author of Genesis.

Date:
Moses likely wrote Genesis during the wilderness wandering (1446-1406 BC).

Theme:
God is the Creator of all things who graciously makes covenants with his people.

Summary:
The story begins with the eternal God creating everything visible in six days. Creation culminates with humanity created in God's image and residing in the Lord's paradise. However, man rebels against the Creator God. A salvation promise is made and so begins the story of redemption. God makes a gracious covenant with Abraham, promising land, offspring, and blessing. As the story unfolds, Abraham's family begins to grow. The story starts with two people in Eden and concludes with seventy people fleeing a famine arriving in Egypt.

Key Passages:
In the beginning, God created the heavens and the earth (1:1).

I will put enmity between you and the woman, and between your offspring and her offspring; he shall bruise your head, and you shall bruise his heel (3:15).

Now the Lord said to Abram, "Go from your country and your kindred and your father's house to the land that I will show you. And I will make of you a great nation, and I will bless you and make your name great, so that you will be a blessing. I will bless those who bless you, and him who dishonors you I will curse, and in you all the families of the earth shall be blessed (12:1-3).

The scepter shall not depart from Judah, nor the ruler's staff from between his feet, until tribute comes to him; and to him shall be the obedience of the peoples (49:10).

Christ Connection:
Jesus is the Seed of the woman who will crush the head of the serpent. The covenant promise made to Abraham finds its fulfillment in Jesus.

Application:
Anyone can trace the answers to why things are how they are today back to Genesis. Even as humankind rebels against God, God is merciful and gracious. He is a promise-making God who never breaks his word. As you see the struggle of sin around you and in you, remember that God promised victory through the Seed of the woman. That Seed is Jesus Christ, who has come and crushed the head of the serpent to secure eternal salvation for all who will believe. Although battles are won and lost, the victory is secure. Be encouraged that the all-powerful Creator God loves you with everlasting love.

EXODUS

Author:
Moses is the author of Exodus.

Date:
Exodus, like Genesis, was written after the Israelites departed from Egypt and lived in the wilderness (1446-1406 BC).

Theme:
God hears his people's cries, responds in power, and desires to make himself known. God's grace in redemption and presence runs throughout the book.

Summary:
God hears his people's cries and graciously remembers his promise. God delivers his people by his mighty power. The Passover receives celebration, and God gives Moses the Law. The Mosaic covenant is ratified, but the people still rebel. In rebellion, the Israelites make a golden calf and worship it. Moses intercedes and offers himself as a substitute for the people. God shows his mercy and reveals himself more significantly to Moses, and the book concludes with the construction of the Tabernacle.

Key Passages:
Their cry for rescue from slavery came up to God. And God heard their groaning, and God remembered his covenant with Abraham, with Issac, and with Jacob (2:23c-24).

But for this purpose I have raised you, to show you my power, so that my name may be proclaimed in all the earth (9:16).

The blood shall be a sign for you on the houses where you are. And when I see the blood, I will pass over you, and no plague will befall you to destroy you, when I strike the land of Egypt (12:13).

The LORD passed before him and proclaimed, The LORD, the LORD, a God merciful and gracious, slow to anger, and abounding in steadfast love and faithfulness, keeping steadfast love for thousands, forgiving iniquity and transgression and sin, but who will by no means clear the guilty, visiting the iniquity of the fathers on the children and the children's children, to the third and the fourth generation (34.6-7).

Christ Connection:
Jesus is the Passover lamb without a spot or blemish that secures salvation by his blood. He is also the perfect law keeper who fulfills every command.

Application:
God hears his people's cries. You can trust the God who hears, knows, and acts for his people. God is also gracious and kind toward those who trust in him. Put your confidence in his consistent and constant care. Rejoice that God forgives your sin and charges your guilt to the Passover Lamb. Furthermore, God gives his gracious Law, so we know what he requires of his people. He desires to dwell among his people. Remember, the law is good as it reveals God's righteous character. Although we break that law, Jesus Christ kept the righteous requirements and his obedience is credited to us as righteousness through faith.

LEVITICUS

Author:
Moses is the primary author of Leviticus.

Date:
Leviticus continues the story of Exodus, written during the wilderness wandering in the 15th century BC.

Theme:
God is holy, and his holiness requires the atonement for sin so that his presence can be among his people.

Summary:
The LORD is holy and calls Israel to be holy. Israel was to reflect who God is to the world around them. They were to be set apart people. God graciously gives the sacrificial system that demonstrates what he requires from his people. God is both the author and receiver of true worship. The day of atonement lies at the very heart of the book as a reminder that the priest must shed animal blood for the forgiveness of sins. After making atonement, God tells his people how they should conduct themselves.

Key Passages:
Among those who are near me I will be sanctified, and before all the people I will be glorified (10:3).

Then he shall go out to the altar that is before the LORD and make atonement for it, and shall take some of the blood of the bull and some of the goat, and put it on the horns of the altar all around. And he shall sprinkle some of the blood on it with his finger seven times, and cleanse it and consecrate it from the uncleannesses of the people of Israel (16:18-19).

You shall not take vengeance or bear a grudge against the sons of your own people, but you shall love your neighbor as yourself: I am the LORD (19:18).

Consecrate yourselves, therefore, and be holy, for I am the LORD your God. Keep my statues and do them; I am the LORD who sanctifies you (20:7-8).

Christ Connection:
The Day of Atonement was only a shadow of what was to come. Jesus offering himself as the final sacrifice for sins, substituting for sinners and bearing their guilt.

Application:
Leviticus reminds us of the holiness of God and the separation sinful humans have from him. Yet, despite our sinfulness, God desires to be in a relationship with us. We can delight in the God who draws near to us and provides the way of redemption through atonement. We must remember that our behavior results from God's grace shown to us. We cannot earn God's favor, but once we receive it in Christ, we are to love him and our neighbor as ourselves. The bloodiness of the sacrifical system shows us how bad sin is. As the redeemed of God let us renounce and run from the sin that Jesus bled and died for.

NUMBERS

Author:
Moses is the primary author of Numbers.

Date:
Numbers chronicles the wilderness wandering, written in the 15th century BC.

Theme:
Sin has severe consequences, and God will judge accordingly. However, God will raise a faithful generation who will trust and obey.

Summary:
The people of God begin the wilderness wandering that lasts forty years. The LORD reveals his glory through judgment upon Israel's rebellion. Israel's complaints, distrust, and disobedience all resulted in the first generation of Israel not entering the promised land. God's promise to Abraham of blessing gets observed through Baalam, who cannot but speak blessing over the people of God. Despite the failures of God's people, he remains faithful to his promise of bringing them into the land after the original generation dies. God will not revoke his promise to Abraham.

Key Passages:
The LORD bless you and keep you; the LORD make his face to shine upon you and be gracious to you; the LORD lift up his countenance upon you and give you peace (6:24-26).

But Caleb quieted the people before Moses and said, "Let us go up at once and occupy it, for we are well able to overcome it" (13:30).

So Moses made a bronze serpent and set it on a pole. And if a serpent bit anyone, he would look at the bronze serpent and live (21:9).

I see him, but not now; I behold him, but not near: a star shall come out of Jacob, and a scepter shall rise out of Israel; it shall crush the forehead of Moab and break down all the sons of Sheth (24:17).

Christ Connection:
Just as the bronze serpent was raised in the wilderness, so was Jesus, who was raised on the cross. Baalam foretells of the coming of Jesus.

Application:
Complaining, lacking trust, and disobedience toward God have consequences. When we think about how God has blessed us in Christ, why would we desire to act like the Israelites in the wilderness? A complaining spirit tells God he is not enough and his provision is lacking in our lives. God desires to use people who are satisfied with him and seek to follow his commands. Our motivation comes through the gospel, which changes our lives. Commit yourself to doing these things because of the goodness of God shown to you. Our joy is inseparably linked to our satisfaction in God.

DEUTERONOMY

Author:
Moses wrote the majority of Deuteronomy.

Date:
Deuteronomy is the final book of Moses, written at the end of the 15th century BC.

Theme:
Deuteronomy means "second law." There will be blessings for covenant obedience and curses for covenant disobedience.

Summary:
The LORD is the absolute ruler of Israel, and under his rule and reign, Israel will experience blessings for obedience and curses for disobedience. Love for God is supposed to motivate covenant obedience. Deuteronomy also points forward to a future prophet who will be greater than Moses and will come and speak in the name of the LORD. The book ends with Moses' death outside the land of promise and the people, under the leadership of Joshua, poised to take the land God was giving them.

Key Passages:
Hear, O Israel: The LORD our God, the LORD is one. You shall love the LORD your God with all your heart and with all your soul and with all your might (6:4-5).

And if you faithfully obey the voice of the LORD your God, being careful to do all his commandments that I command you today, the LORD your God will set you high above all the nations of the earth (28:1)

But if you will not obey the voice of the LORD your God or be careful to do all his commandments and his statutes that I command you today, then all these curses shall come upon you and overtake you (28:15).

And the LORD your God will circumcise your heart and the heart of your offspring so that you will love the LORD your God with all your heart and with all your soul, that you may live (30:6).

Christ Connection:
Jesus is the new and better prophet Moses predicted would come after him (Deut 18:18). Jesus is the covenant keeper and faithfully fulfilled Deuteronomy.

Application:
No matter how hard we try, we cannot keep God's Law with our power. We need Another, and that is precisely what Jesus is. We receive the covenant blessings because Jesus secured them for us. The Law is good, and the Gospel is greater. Worship the Lord because Jesus secured your blessing by giving you his. Give thanks for the forgiveness of sins. Walk in obedience because God has enabled you to do so through his power. Delight in God for he has shown great mercy. God's love for you is an everlasting love without beginning or end. The reason God will never stop loving you is because he never started, he just always has.

JONATHAN SOLE

THE PROPHETS

JOSHUA

Author:
Joshua wrote significant portions, probably completed by another inspired author, sometime from David to Solomon.

Date:
Joshua is a recounting of the conquest and ends with his death sometime in the 14th century BC.

Theme:
God delivers on his promise to Abraham through the conquest and secures victory for his people.

Summary:
Joshua accounts for the second generation's conquest of the promised land after the Exodus. What God promised, he fulfilled. Part of God's covenant with Abraham finds its completion in Israel, which inhabits the promised land. However, their blessing in the land is conditional and depends on covenant faithfulness. Joshua is an optimistic book in which Joshua secured significant victories, and the people trusted in the LORD and served him faithfully. The book ends with Joshua's death, and Israel enters a new era.

Key Passages:
This Book of the Law shall not depart from your mouth, but you shall meditate on it day and night, so that you may be careful to do according to all that is written in it. For then you will make your way prosperous, and then you will have good success. Have I not commanded you? Be strong and courageous. Do not be frightened, and do not be dismayed, for the LORD

your God is with you wherever you go (1:8-9).

Not one word of all the good promises that the LORD had made to the house of Israel had failed; all came to pass (21:45).

Choose this day whom you will serve...But as for me and my house, we will serve the LORD (24:15).

Christ Connection:
Jesus is the Commander of the LORD's army who secures victory for his people by subduing his adversaries.

Application:
God desires to put courage in our hearts. We know that in this life, we will face obstacles and opposition. We must remember that we are more than conquerors through him who loved us. While battles may be fierce, our strength and confidence rest in the fact that the Commander of the LORD's army goes before us and has surrounded us in his grace. This encouragement is what we need to press on in faith and obedience. Since we receive encouragement, we need to look out for fellow brothers and sisters who are weary and give them the same encouragement. The war is over, Satan is defeated, and we live as victors in Christ. May we continue to persevere until that final day and the kingdom is experienced in it's fullness.

JUDGES

Author:
Anonymous – Some traditions ascribe their final composition to Samuel.

Date:
The book of Judges spans roughly 400 years and concludes around 1050 BC.

Theme:
Sin plagues the human condition and brings about God's judgment. Yet, even through judgment, God is gracious to his people.

Summary:
While in the land of promise and prospering numerically, Israel turns away from covenant obedience in times of comfort only to bring judgment upon themselves. The people experience the curses of Deuteronomy because they disobeyed the LORD. After a season of affliction, God graciously sends judges (saviors) to rescue the people. The problem for Israel is that they needed a heart change because external conformity would never work. The depravity of humanity manifests itself in that everyone does what is right in their own eyes.

Key Passages:
And there arose another generation after them who did not know the LORD or the work that he had done for Israel. And the people of Israel did what was evil in the sight of the LORD and served Baals (2:10-11).

So, the people of Israel lived among the Canaanites, the Hittites, the Amorites, the Perizzites, the Hivites, and the Jebusites. And their daughters they took to themselves for wives, and their own daughters they gave to their sons, and they served their gods (3:5-6).

And the people of Israel cried out to the LORD, saying, "We have sinned against you because we have forsaken our God and have served the Baals" (10:10).

In those days there was no king in Israel. Everyone did what was right in his own eyes (21:25)

Christ Connection:
Jesus is the true and everlasting Judge/King that the people of God need to live in the kingdom.

Application:
Judges is a dark reminder that when we forget God's word and ways, we open ourselves up to great trouble. If we surround ourselves with worldliness, it is only a matter of time before we end up like it. Our world today is filled with moral relativism, and everyone does what is right in their own eyes. We must hold to objective morality, read God's Law, and see Jesus in it. We see that God will discipline wickedness but not forsake his people. God remains faithful to his promises even when his people fail him. Because we have God's Word and his Spirit dwells within us we are not left to our own devices. In these days the King is on the throne and he has enabled us to do right in his eyes.

1&2 SAMUEL

Author:
The author is anonymous, although many believe that Samuel contributed significantly to the early parts of the story. An inspired author likely completed the final form around the 6th century BC.

Date:
Samuel spans from around 1100 B.C. to 971 BC. It was completed sometime after the death of David.

Theme:
God is the supreme monarch over Israel and raises whom he wills to rule and lead his people.

Summary:
The reign of the Judges ended because Israel wanted a king like the other nations. The monarchy begins with Saul, a wicked king, and Samuel ends with David, a man after God's own heart. God's choice is not based upon outward attributes but inward character. Central to the message of Samuel is God's covenant with David, where he promises to establish an eternal kingdom through David's offspring. However, even King David fails, showing the need for a Righteous King who does not fail.

Key Passages:
"The LORD will judge the ends of the earth; he will give strength to his king and exalt the horn of his anointed" (1 Sam. 2:10).
But the people refused to obey the voice of Samuel. And they said, "No! But there shall be a king over us, that we also may be like all the nations and that our king may judge us and go out

before us and fight our battles" (1 Sam. 8:19-20).

"For the LORD sees not as man sees: man looks on the outward appearance, but the LORD looks on the heart" (1 Sam. 16:7)

I will raise up your offspring after you, who shall come from your body, and I will establish his kingdom...And your house and your kingdom shall be made sure forever before me (2 Sam 7:12,16).

Christ Connection:
Jesus is the promised King who will come from the line of David and whose kingdom will never end. He is genuinely the one after God's own heart.

Application:
1&2 Samuel shows the danger of trying to be like the world around us. God's plan and provision are better than anything this world offers. Sometimes, what we think or who we think might be best is not God's choice. Despite our stubbornness, God redeems wicked desires and uses them for his glory and our good. Yet even the godly can fall into egregious sins if they are not careful to guard their hearts and stay near the Lord. A true mark of the follower of God is observed in their repentance when confronted with their sin. Pray for a sensitive heart, and do not allow the little sins to compound and lead to severe consequences in this life. We too want to be described as men and women after God's own heart.

1 & 2 KINGS

Author:
No single author but multiple compositions were compiled by inspired men to provide the completed form.

Date:
Kings lasted from roughly 970 BC to 561 BC., so no single human author could exist.

Theme:
God will not tolerate prolonged unfaithfulness. Israel's idolatry ultimately leads to exile from the land of promise.

Summary:
After David's death, Solomon takes the throne. He builds the temple and starts strong but finishes unfaithful. The kingdom divides, and God raises prophets to turn the people back from idol worship. Eventually, both kingdoms fall, and the nation of Israel is exiled. The curses in Deuteronomy for breaking the covenant are actualized in Kings. The book's conclusion, however, leaves a glimmer of hope as King Jehoiachin is released from prison and dines with the king of Babylon; David's offspring is still alive.

Key Passages:
O LORD, God of Israel, there is no God like you, in heaven above or on earth beneath, keeping covenant and showing steadfast love to your servants who walk before you with all their heart" (8:23).

"How long will you go limping between two different opinions? If the LORD is God, follow him; but if Baal, then follow

him" (18:21).

In the ninth year of Hoshea, the king of Assyria captured Samaria, and he carried the Israelites away to Assyria and placed them in Halah...And this occurred because the people of Israel had sinned against the LORD their God (2 Kings 17:6-7).

And Nebuchadnezzar king of Babylon came to the city while his servants were besieging it, and Jehoiachin the king of Judah gave himself and his mother and his servants and his palace officials (24:11-12)

Christ Connection:
Jesus is the perfect King of Kings who righteously leads his people from exile into the eternal promised land.

Application:
Kings shows the steady and sure decline when people turn away from God. God's kindness and patience are means to lead to repentance, but for Israel and Judah, they forsook the Lord and continued in idolatry. Even as disciples of Jesus, we can experience consequences for our sinful choices. We should not presume upon God's grace but seek to walk in it as we pursue obedience to Jesus. Our hope is that the Son of David rules and reigns as King of Kings in our hearts. His rule is everlasting and the day is coming when he will make right all that is wrong in the new heavens and earth.

JEREMIAH

Author:
The priest and prophet Jeremiah authored the book.

Date:
Jeremiah covers the time of 627 BC to the temple's destruction in 587 BC The appendix at the end of chapter 52 is dated 561 BC.

Theme:
Jeremiah proclaims a message of judgment for sin but also looks forward to future salvation.

Summary:
Jeremiah's ministry takes place during the reign of Josiah (627 BC) in Judah. His call is to warn the people of coming judgment if they do not repent and return to God. The people fail and are sent into a 70-year exile. Jeremiah provides further commentary on the prophetic words given during 2 Kings. Sadly, Jeremiah witnesses the destruction of both the temple and Jerusalem. Breaking the covenant made at Sinai leads to judgment and exile. But the LORD will make a new covenant with his people that sinners cannot break and deal permanently with sins through complete forgiveness.

Key Passages:
"Behold, I have put my words in your mouth. See, I have set you this day over nations and over kingdoms, to pluck up and to break down, to destroy and to overthrow, to build and to plant" (1:9b-10).

"Let not the wise man boast in his wisdom, let not the mighty man boast in his might, let not the rich man boast in his riches, but let him who boasts boast in this, that he understands and knows me, that I am the LORD who practices steadfast love, justice, and righteousness in the earth" (9:23-24).

"I will raise up for David a righteous Branch, and he shall reign as king and deal wisely and shall execute justice and righteousness in the land" (23:5).

"I will make a new covenant with the house of Israel and the house of Judah...I will be their God, and they shall be my people (31:31,33).

Christ Connection:
Jesus is the Righteous Branch who reigns as king and mediates the New Covenant.

Application:
Judgment for sin comes, but God's final word is salvation through a new and better covenant. God has so loved you that he sent Jesus to secure the promises of the New Covenant by his blood. The present future might look bleak, but we can look beyond what is hard to what is eternal, which is the promise of a permanent dwelling place where we are united in personal fellowship with God. In the new covenant, God writes his law upon our hearts and enables us to walk in communion with him through Jesus by the indwelling Holy Spirit.

EZEKIEL

Author:
The prophet Ezekiel is the writer of the book.

Date:
Ezekiel's prophetic ministry began in exile in 597 BC and spans to approximately 570 BC.

Theme:
God displays his sovereignty through imminent judgment and future grace.

Summary:
The exile has already begun. Jeremiah and Ezekiel likely served together in Jerusalem as priests for a time. Destruction comes to Jerusalem 11 years into Ezekiel's ministry. Ezekiel unlike Jeremiah goes into exile with the people. The glorious presence of the LORD departs from Israel due to the sin of the people. Through God's sovereign judgment, he demonstrates that he alone is the LORD. However, judgment is not the final word. Ezekiel looks forward to the day when the Spirit will indwell his people, and the new creation comes, where the dwelling place of God will be with a man.

Key Passages:
And he said to me, "Son of man, I send you to the people of Israel, to nations of rebels, who have rebelled against me. They and their fathers have transgressed against me to this very day" (2:3).
"Son of man, I have made you a watchman for the house of Israel. Whenever you hear a word from my mouth, you shall

give them warning from me" (3:17).

And I will give you a new heart, and a new spirit I will put within you. And I will remove the heart of stone from your flesh and give you a heart of flesh. And I will put my Spirit within you, and cause you to walk in my statutes and be careful to obey my rules (36:26-27).

"And my holy name I will make known in the midst of my people Israel, and I will not let my holy name be profaned anymore. And the nations shall know that I am the LORD, the Holy One of Israel" (39:7).

Christ Connection:
Jesus is the Son of Man who faithfully speaks all the words of his Father and because of his finish work on the cross, God, by his Spirit, can replace the heart of stone with a heart of flesh.

Application:
Ezekiel, like Jeremiah, reminds us of the severe consequences of sin. We must not forget that while God is a God of grace, he also brings judgment upon all who continue to rebel against him. We see that apart from God's sovereign grace, our hearts will remain stone. Our hope and confidence are not in our abilities or performance but in God's having caused us to be born again according to his mercy. Ultimately, God will dwell with his creation again. Rejoice in a secure salvation.

ISAIAH

Author:
Isaiah, the prophet, wrote the book.

Date:
Isaiah's time began in the reign of Uzziah around 750 BC and ended in either 700 or 680 BC.

Theme:
Isaiah points to the continual need to trust God and warns against the sin of pride and unbelief. He also filled with the gospel of the coming Messiah.

Summary:
Isaiah is like many of the other prophets. He warns the people of their pride, external religion, and unbelief. His continual message is of hope and trust in the LORD. As he foretold, the Northern Kingdom fell to the Assyrians during his ministry. However, all who would turn to the LORD would experience salvation. Isaiah looks forward to a Prince of Peace who is also the Suffering Servant pierced for the transgressions of many. After the Suffering Servant comes renewal, God establishes a new creation of the heavens and earth, and all the inhabitants will dwell together in perfect harmony.

Key Passages:
"Come now, let us reason together, says the LORD: though your sins are like scarlet, they shall be as white as snow; though they are red like crimson, they shall become like wool (1:18).

For to us a child is born, to us a son is given; and the

government shall be upon his shoulder, and his name shall be called Wonderful Counselor, Mighty God, Everlasting Father, Prince of Peace (9:6)

But they who wait for the LORD shall renew their strength; they shall mount up with wings like eagles; they shall run and not be weary; they shall walk and not faint (40:31).

But he was pierced for our transgressions; he was crushed for our iniquities; upon him was the chastisement that brought us peace, and with his wounds we are healed (53:5).

Christ Connection:
Jesus is Immanuel (Is 7:14), the child born as the Prince of Peace (Is 9:6). Jesus is also the Suffering Servant who secures salvation through his death (Is 53).

Application:
Isaiah reminds us of our need to trust God in good or bad times. So much religious practice can become formal and mechanical, not from a renewed heart passionate for Jesus and God's glory. For our worship to stay where God wants it, we must continually gaze upon the Suffering Servant who took our sins away. As we wait, trust, and consider God's good provision, he will renew our strength, and our worship will be with rejoicing. The Gospel gives us an eternal song to sing. We can look forward with expectant hope because of what Jesus accomplished in our place. Chapter 53 is the clearest OT picture of the suffering and triumph of the Messiah.

HOSEA

Author:
Hosea is the author of the book that bears his name.

Date:
Hosea's ministry began around the same time as Amos and went from roughly 760 – 730 BC.

Theme:
Israel's unfaithfulness brings about God's punishment. Hosea points to God's unfailing love for his chosen people.

Summary:
Hosea gives vivid language concerning the Northern Kingdom's unfaithfulness to the LORD. Hosea's marriage to Gomer and the names of their children illustrate the relationship of unfaithful Israel to their God, who loves them fiercely. The LORD declares to them that he is their God and their only savior. While Israel is unfaithful, they are not forsaken, for he will heal them when they return to the LORD in repentance. In God's faithful love for his people, he desires the same single-hearted devotion from his people. Hosea ends with the LORD showing how he delights in mercy and grace through the restoration of his people who behave as an unfaithful wife.

Key Passages:
My people are destroyed for lack of knowledge, because you have rejected knowledge, I reject you from being a priest to me. And since you have forgotten the Law of your God, I also will forget your children (4:6).

"Come, let us return to the LORD; for he has torn us, that he may heal us; he has struck us down, and he will bind us up. After two days he will revive us; on the third day he will raise us up, that we may live before him" (6:1-2).

"When Israel was a child, I loved him, and out of Egypt I called my son" (11:1).

Whoever is wise, let him understand these things; whoever is discerning, let him know them; for the ways of the LORD are right, and the upright walk in them, but transgressors stumble in them (14:9).

Christ Connection:
Hosea writes of a third-day resurrection that finds its fulfillment in the resurrection of Jesus from the dead (Hos 6:2). It is Jesus who dies to redeem his wayward bride.

Application:
God desires faithful allegiance, which is manifest in loving obedience. Yet even when we sin and share our affections with what God has forbidden, he remains steadfast in his love toward us. He is the faithful one who continually calls his people to return to him so he might restore them. God delights in forgiving the unfaithful. When you sin, do not try to hide or stay distant; run to God, the lover of your soul, who forgives. It is the Lord's kindness that leads to repentance.

JOEL

Author:
Joel, the son of Pethuel, is the author.

Date:
The certainty concerning the date of authorship is unknown. The lack of mention of the Syrians or Babylonians makes it likely that Joel could have written in the 8th century BC.

Theme:
Joel makes a heartfelt plea for repentance before the Day of the Lord, which refers to final judgment and restoration.

Summary:
Joel begins by describing a swarm of locusts destroying the land and the need for the people to repent. The same repeated pattern occurs in the second chapter, where judgment precedes and prompts repentance from the LORD's people. God desires true, heartfelt repentance through a rendered heart. Later, God will pour out his Spirit on all flesh; all who call upon the name of the LORD shall be saved. Peter recognizes this event to take place at Pentecost forty days after the resurrection. Then a final judgment of all the nations will occur.

Key Passages:
Consecrate a fast; call a solemn assembly. Gather the elders and all the inhabitants of the land to the house of the LORD your God and cry out to the LORD (1:14).

"Yet even now," declares the LORD, return to me with all your

heart, with fasting, with weeping, and with mourning; and rend your hearts and not your garments" (2:12-13).

"And it shall come to pass afterward, that I will pour out my Spirit on all flesh; your sons and your daughters shall prophesy, your old men shall dream dreams, and your young men shall see visions (2:28).

"And it shall come to pass that everyone who calls on the name of the LORD shall be saved (2:31).

Christ Connection:
Jesus is the name that all people must call on for salvation. God has given him the name above everyone, and there is no other name by which people can be saved.

Application:
God wants his people to walk in fellowship, obedience, and wholeness. Chasing after sinful and lesser things displeases God and settles for a life of difficulty. God will judge wickedness but restore his children who come to him in sincerity of heart. Let us celebrate repentance. A day is coming when God will judge the world in righteousness and end all our sins and difficulties. Joel gives a message of the future and final hope. Until that day, let us be wise in our dealings and sensitive in our hearts toward God and others.

AMOS

Author:
Amos, who was a farmer called to prophesy, wrote the book.

Date:
Amos wrote during the reign of Uzziah in Judah and Jeroboam in Israel (793-740 BC).

Theme:
Amos warns against injustice, hypocrisy, and God's faithfulness to remember his covenant.

Summary:
The LORD judges the nations around Judah and Israel but also judges his people for their sins. Israel is guilty of oppressing people experiencing poverty and deserting their religion. The LORD despises Israel's hypocrisy and will not accept their worship while practicing evil and promoting injustice. He was not quick to exile his people, but after constant warnings and more minor consequences for disobedience, Israel continued in hardhearted ways. However, the end for God's people is not destruction but final restoration.

Key Passages:
"For three transgressions of Israel, and for four, I will not revoke the punishment, because they sell the righteous for silver, and the needy for a pair of sandals" (2:6).

Seek good, and not evil, that you may live; and so the LORD, the God of hosts, will be with you, as you have said. Hate evil, *and love good, and establish justice in the gate; it may be that the LORD, the God of hosts, will be gracious to the remnant of Joseph (5:14-15).*

But let justice roll down like waters, and righteousness like an ever-flowing stream (5:24).

"In that day I will raise up the booth of David that is fallen and repair its breaches, and raise up its ruins and rebuild it as in the days of old" (9:11).

Christ Connection:
Jesus is the prophet who speaks God's message of life and receives rejection like Amos.

Application:
Amos shows us how much God cares about the two greatest commandments: love God and love people. Israel's problem was in their failure to do both. The reality is we can only do one with the other. We demonstrate our love for God in our worship and obedience to him and our love and care for others. We should not be complacent regarding oppression and injustice, but with compassion, we must seek to help the poor and needy. It is always our love for God because of Christ that fuels our passion for people. Justice and compassion flow downstream from the Gospel.

OBADIAH

Author:
Obadiah wrote the short book that bears his name.

Date:
Obadiah was written soon after the destruction of Jerusalem (586 BC) and during the Babylonian exile.

Theme:
God is sovereign over all nations and judges the nations that mistreat others.

Summary:
Obadiah is the most miniature book in the Old Testament. It denounces Edom for mistreating Judah during the destruction of Jerusalem and the Babylonian exile. The Edomites are the descendants of Esau, and instead of being an ally to Judah, they were enemies as well. God promises to humble and punish the enemies of his people. A coming Day of the LORD is near when judgment comes upon the ungodly. The LORD's judgment upon the wicked also results in the salvation and restoration of his people. In God's restoration, the establishment of his kingdom lasts forever.

Key Passages:
Will I not on that day, declares the LORD, destroy the wise men out of Edom, and understanding out of Mount Esau? (8).

But do not gloat over the day of your brother in the day of his misfortune; do not rejoice over the people of Judah in the day of their ruin; do not boast in the day of distress (12).

For the day of the LORD is near upon all the nations. As you have done, it shall be done to you; your deeds shall return on your head (15).

Saviors shall go up to Mount Zion to rule Mount Esau, and the kingdom shall be the LORD's (21).

Christ Connection:
Jesus is the judge of all the earth. On the Day of the LORD, he will execute perfect justice upon the ungodly and final salvation for his people.

Application:
Although Obadiah is the most miniature book in the Old Testament, it has a big message for readers today. As New Covenant believers, we recognize some discontinuity from Old Testament Israel but see God's protection of his people against their enemies. Obadiah reminds us that the wicked may prosper for a time, but righteousness and justice will eventually reign. The Lord will vindicate his people on the day of judgment. God will always keep his promises, and our assurance is that a future and final salvation will come. Until that day, let us seek to do good and not harm the household of faith, our brothers and sisters in Christ.

JONAH

Author:
Jonah, the son of Amittai, is the author.

Date:
Jonah lived and ministered during the reign of Jeroboam II (793-753 BC).

Theme:
God is sovereign over his messenger and his message. His message of salvation is for everyone.

Summary:
The book of Jonah focuses far more on the messenger than the message and outcome. It is a story of rebellion, salvation, ethnic prejudice, and the LORD's compassion for the helpless. Jonah flees from the presence of the LORD and sets sail west when God calls him to go east. During an epic storm at sea, Jonah offers to be thrown into the ocean to calm the storm of God's wrath. A great fish swallows him and he spends three days in the belly of the fish. After his rescue from the fish, he obeys God and proclaims God's message of repentance to the Ninevites. Once they repent, Jonah reveals that he wanted them judged and knew God is merciful and gracious and grants repentance to the wicked.

Key Passages:
And the LORD appointed a great fish to swallow up Jonah. And Jonah was in the belly of the fish three days and three nights (1:17).

"But I with the voice of thanksgiving will sacrifice to you; what

I have vowed I will pay. Salvation belongs to the LORD" (2:9).

When God saw what they did, how they turned from their evil way, God relented of the disaster that he had said he would do to them, and he did not do it (3:10).

"And should not I pity Nineveh, that great city, in which there are more than 120,000 persons who do not know their right hand from their left, and also much cattle? (4:11).

Christ Connection:
Jesus, like Jonah, was sacrificed to appease God's wrath against sin. Just as Jonah was in the belly of the fish for three days, so too was Jesus in the tomb.

Application:
Jonah warns us against running away from God's call on our lives. Ethnic prejudice is not tolerated in the Christian faith; the gospel message is for everyone without distinction. Jonah is an example of what not to be in our service to Jesus. Furthermore, we see God's heart for little children who do not know what sin is. His protection is for the young and incapable of understanding. Ultimately, God is gracious and delights in the salvation of the outsider. God's grace is mysterious and surprising at times. We cannot predict to whom or where it will go. As followers of Jesus we must be faithful in sharing the gospel to all people without distinction. Heaven is filled with people from every tribe, tongue, and nation.

MICAH

Author:
Micah of Moresheth is the author.

Date:
Micah prophesied during the reign of Jotham, Ahaz, and Hezekiah in the Southern Kingdom (740-690 BC).

Theme:
Micah warns the wealthy about oppressing the poor and the judgment to come. However, God is bringing salvation.

Summary:
Micah's ministry is at the same time as Isaiah's; therefore, they have similar rebukes and warnings for the people of Judah. The people of Judah enjoyed a time of prosperity, and as a result, the wealthy neglected the poor and abused justice. God will not allow covenant disobedience to continue. Micah warns of coming judgment where Israel will fall, and Jerusalem will become a heap of ruins. The Northern Kingdom falls during the ministry of Micah (722 BC). God's final word, however, is not destruction but salvation. Micah, like Isaiah, looks forward to a day of renewal, and all the people will worship the LORD through a Ruler who is to come from Bethlehem.

Key Passages:
Woe to those who devise wickedness and work evil on their beds! When the morning dawns, they perform it, because it is in the power of their hand" (2:1).

But you, O Bethlehem Ephrathah, who are too little to be

among the clans of Judah, from you shall come forth for me one who is to be ruler in Israel, whose coming forth is from of old, from ancient days (5:2).

He has told you, O man, what is good; and what does the LORD require of you but to do justice, and to love kindness, and to walk humbly with your God? (6:8).

Christ Connection:
Jesus is the promised one who will come from Bethlehem and rule Israel. The story of his coming continues since the promise in the Garden of Eden.

Application:
Micah shows us a trap that comes with prosperity, neglecting the needs of others and becoming complacent in our devotion to God. As followers of Jesus, we are to do justice, love kindness, and walk humbly before our God. We do this when we give from our abundance to the less fortunate and genuinely love the mercy shown. Micah also reminds us that God is faithful to his promises, and the Seed of the Woman is coming from Bethlehem to crush the head of the serpent. God has promised to cast all our sins into the depths of the sea because Jesus has paid the debt owed. We live without the fear of condemnation. Rejoice in forgiveness, seek to do good, be a blessing and not a burden to those in your life.

NAHUM

Author:
Nahum of Elkosh is the author.

Date:
Nahum comes roughly a century after Jonah, sometime between 660 and 612 BC.

Theme:
God is sovereign and will punish those who refuse to repent.

Summary:
Nahum can be considered the sequel to Jonah concerning Nineveh. When Jonah preached repentance to the people, they turned and received forgiveness. Nahum tells the very opposition story. Roughly 100 years later, Nineveh is now facing the wrath of God for their return to wickedness. Nahum speaks to the people of Judah and rejoices in God's justice and judgment upon the wicked and oppressive Assyrians, where Nineveh was the capital. Nahum foretells Assyria's destruction from the Babylonians in 612 BC. The message is clear: God will not tolerate prolonged wickedness, and the Lord's justice will come with a vengeance upon the ungodly.

Key Passages:
The LORD is a jealous and avenging God; the LORD is avenging and wrathful; the LORD takes vengeance on his adversaries and keeps wrath for his enemies. The LORD is slow to anger and great in power, and the LORD will by no means clear the guilty (1:2-3).

The LORD is good, a stronghold in the day of trouble; he knows those who take refuge in him (1:7).

Behold, upon the mountains, the feet of him who brings good news, who publishes peace! (1:15).

Your shepherds are asleep, O king of Assyria; your nobles slumber. Your people are scattered on the mountains with none to gather them. There is no easing your hurt; your wound is grievous. All who hear the news about you clap their hands over you. For upon whom has not come your unceasing evil? (3:18-19).

Christ Connection:
Nahum promises good news of peace through the LORD's salvation of his people, which Jesus ultimately fulfills.

Application:
Nahum reminds us of God's righteousness and justice. God takes no pleasure in the death of the wicked, but he receives glory in his justice. Nahum also reminds us that revivals are often short-lived experiences. We shouldn't chase after revivals or experiences. Within a couple of generations, Nineveh returned to its old ways. As followers of Jesus, we must continue to teach and train the next generation lest we, too, fall into the pattern of the Ninevites. One generation is responsible for reaching the next generation (See Psalm 145).

HABAKKUK

Author:
Habakkuk is the author of the book.

Date:
Habakkuk was written sometime in the 7th century (640-615 BC).

Theme:
Habakkuk wrestles with how God can use wicked nations to accomplish his purposes. He ultimately rests in God's sovereignty and goodness.

Summary:
Habakkuk opens by asking God why bad things are happening all around him. The startling thing is that God tells Habakkuk that he is raising the Chaldeans (Babylonians) to overthrow Assyria and Judah. Habakkuk can hardly believe what he hears, and the LORD tells him to wait. Salvation is coming, and the righteous shall live by faith. Eventually, even the Chaldeans suffer defeat, and the LORD will send his people back to rebuild. Although Habakkuk struggles to understand now, he takes joy in the God of his salvation and trusts that the LORD's work is proper. His prayer at the end of the book demonstrates his resolve to trust despite the physical circumstances.

Key Passages:
O LORD, how long shall I cry for help, and you will not hear? Or cry to you "Violence!" and you will not save? (1:2).

"Behold, his soul is puffed up; it is not upright within him, but

the righteous shall live by faith" (2:4).

Though the fig tree should not blossom, nor fruit be on the vines, the produce of the olive fail and the fields yield no food, the flock be cut off from the fold and there be no herd in the stalls, yet I will rejoice in the LORD; I will take joy in the God of my salvation. God, the Lord, is my strength; he makes my feet like the deer's; he makes me tread on my high places (3:17-19).

Christ Connection:
Habakkuk's statement concerning the righteous living by faith looks forward to Jesus. Jesus supplies the perfect righteousness that his people receive by grace through faith.

Application:
Habakkuk gives us a timeless and essential message. We must know it is okay to ask God why bad things happen to us or around us. Sometimes, the Lord gives us a clear answer, but other times, we must wait and trust in him. Habakkuk teaches us how to respond honestly to God in times of great uncertainty and deep distress. We might lose our health, a loved one, or some other tragedy that comes our way, but we can rest assured that God will be our strength, and we can find joy in his salvation despite the circumstances. Habakkuk is a book of hope during very dark times. Be encouraged in your struggle; God is good, and he is saving you.

ZEPHANIAH

Author:
Zephaniah, the son of Cushi, is the author.

Date:
Zephaniah prophesied during the reign of Josiah, the king of Judah (640-610 BC).

Theme:
The Day of the Lord is coming when judgment will be pronounced on all nations, and God will save his people.

Summary:
Zephaniah predicts a coming judgment upon Judah and Jerusalem. While King Josiah made good reforms in Judah, their idolatry brought the LORD's displeasure, and shortly after Zephaniah's time as prophet, Babylon overthrew the Southern Kingdom. Judah's failure to keep the covenant resulted in the exile of the land, just as Moses said. The LORD's judgment is not for Judah only but for all the earth's inhabitants. The Day of the Lord is the day of future judgment, and Zephaniah calls on people to seek the LORD before the day of judgment. Zephaniah sees a day when all peoples will call upon the name of the LORD. God will restore and exalt his people among all the nations of the earth.

Key Passages:
Be silent before the Lord God! For the day of the LORD is near, the LORD has prepared a sacrifice and consecrated his guests (1:7).

I will bring distress on mankind so that they shall walk like the blind because they have sinned against the LORD; their blood shall be poured out like dust, and their flesh like dung (1:17).

Seek the LORD, all you humble of the land, who do his just commands, seek righteousness; seek humility; perhaps you may be hidden on the day of the anger of the LORD (2:3).

The LORD your God is in your midst, a mighty one who will save; he will rejoice over you with gladness; he will quiet you by his love; he will exult over you with loud singing (3:17).

Christ Connection:
Jesus is the judge who will return on the day of judgment and execute justice upon the nations.

Application:
A day is coming when Jesus will return, and the Day of the Lord will arrive. As believers, we do not fear a judgment of separation, but we do have those in our lives that will on that day. The certainty of God's coming judgment should build a sense of urgency to share the Gospel of Jesus Christ. Zephaniah reminds us that God calls on the humble to seek him and flee from the wrath to come. Judgment is a sobering reality of the holiness of God. We are safe because God provided us with Jesus. We do not want to become complacent nor grow comfortable with the reality of coming judgment. Pray for a missional mindset as we move closer to that day as time marches on.

HAGGAI

Author:
Haggai, the prophet, is the author.

Date:
Haggai's ministry came after the people of Judah returned from exile in the second year of Darius I (520 BC).

Theme:
The rebuilding of the temple signifies God's desired presence among his people.

Summary:
Haggai is the first of three post-exilic prophets. Once the first wave of exiles returned to Jerusalem in 538 B.C., they began working to rebuild the temple. It did not take long for them to give up on their task and focus on their dwelling places. The LORD speaks through Haggai and commands them to continue to rebuild the temple. The people were encouraged to look past the present difficulty and see the glory of the LORD in the new temple. God promised them future glory and blessing because he was faithful to his covenant promises. Zerubbabel, the governor of Judah, was chosen by the LORD to lead his people. Zerubbabel, the descendant of David, reassured the promise of a future king.

Key Passages:
"Is it a time for you yourselves to dwell in your paneled houses, while this house lies in ruins? Now, therefore, thus says the LORD of hosts: Consider your ways" (1:4-5).

Then Zerubbabel the son of Shealtiel, and Joshua the son of Jehozadak, the high priest, with all the remnant of the people, obeyed the voice of the LORD their God, and the words of Haggai the prophet, as the LORD their God had sent him. And the people feared the LORD (1:12).

"The latter glory of this house shall be greater than the former, says the LORD of hosts. And in this place I will give peace, declares the LORD of hosts" (2:9).

On that day, declares the LORD of hosts, I will take you, O Zerubbabel my servant, the son of Shealtiel, declares the LORD, and make you like a signet ring, for I have chosen you, declares the LORD of hosts (2:23).

Christ Connection:
Jesus is the promised Seed of the woman who will reign on David's throne, and God has chosen Zerubbabel to continue that Godly lineage.

Application:
Haggai reminds us not to be slothful in the work of the Lord. God desires us to work diligently for his glory. Practically, this means what we start we should finish. As Christians, we recognize we are the temple where God's presence dwells, so we must stay pure and reflect God's glory to the world around us.

ZECHARIAH

Author:
Zechariah, the son of Berechiah, is the author.

Date:
Zechariah spoke simultaneously as Haggai (520-516 BC).

Theme:
While Haggai encouraged the people to rebuild the temple, Zechariah called upon them to repent and return to the Lord. The Day of the Lord is coming upon all nations.

Summary:
Zechariah is the second prophetic book written after the exile. Work on the temple resumes, but the people fall into the old pattern of oppression and injustice. Not even a nearly rebuilt temple and a return to Jerusalem is enough; they need their hearts changed. Amid the call for repentance, Zechariah foretells a future king who will enter Jerusalem on a donkey, bringing salvation for the LORD's people. There will be one that is pierced, and all who gaze upon Him will mourn, and on that day, a fountain opens for the cleansing of sin and uncleanness. Zechariah ends with a message of triumph and victory on the Day of the Lord.

Key Passages:
Not by might, nor by power, but by my Spirit, says the LORD of hosts (4:6b).

Rejoice greatly, O daughter of Zion! Shout aloud, O daughter of Jerusalem! Behold, your king is coming to you; righteous and having salvation is he, humble and mounted on a donkey, on a colt, the foal of a donkey (9:9).

"And I will pour out on the house of David and the inhabitants of Jerusalem a spirit of grace and pleas for mercy, so that, when they look on me, on him whom they have pierced, they shall mourn for him, as one mourns for an only child, and weep bitterly over him, as one weeps over a firstborn" (12:10).

On that day his feet shall stand on the Mount of Olives that lies before Jerusalem on the east, and the Mount of Olives shall be split in two from east to west by a very wide valley (14:4a).

Christ Connection:
Jesus is the humble king who rides in on a donkey. He is the one who is pierced and opens the fountain of forgiveness and washing away of sin.

Application:
Zechariah gives us hope about Jesus' reign and rule. God's promises made in the Old Testament are his promises kept in the New Testament. Jesus was pierced for our sins, and the fountain of forgiveness flows from his blood shed on the cross. Find your assurance by looking to Jesus, who suffered crucifixion, for your salvation. Be faithful in your dealings with others, knowing that you are now an ambassador for Jesus today. Rest in the promise of final victory when our Savior returns to take us home with him.

MALACHI

Author:
Malachi is the author.

Date:
Malachi was the last inspired Old Testament writer and the third and final book written after their return from exile. It was written sometime between 460 – 420 BC.

Theme:
Malachi is concerned with a corrupt priesthood, increasing wickedness in Judah, and robbing God of tithes.

Summary:
Malachi is the last prophet to write, and things do not look good for Judah. The messianic age never came with the rebuilding of the temple, and the people began falling back into the pattern of their ancestors. The problem of internal wickedness persists, and no external reform will accomplish what needs to be done. The priesthood is corrupt and greedy, and the people of Judah are practicing liberal divorce. The people are also cutting back and not tithing as commanded. God would rather then shut the door of the temple than continue to offer their profane worship. Israel is a mess, and Malachi closes with the promise that God will send Elijah, the prophet, to the people and call for their repentance.

Key Passages:
For from the rising of the sun to its setting my name will be great among the nations, and in every place incense will be offered to my name, and a pure offering. For my name will be

great among the nations, says the LORD of hosts (1:11).

"For the man who does not love his wife but divorces her, says the LORD, the God of Israel, covers his garment with violence, says the LORD of hosts" (2:16).

"Bring the full tithe into the storehouse, that there may be food in my house. And thereby put me to the test, says the LORD of hosts, if I will not open the windows of heaven for you and pour down for you a blessing until there is no more need" (3:10).

"Behold, I will send you Elijah the prophet before that great and awesome day of the LORD comes" (4:5).

Christ Connection:
Jesus is the messenger whose way is prepared by another. And when he comes, he is a refiner and will purify his people.

Application:
Malachi is relevant to us today in many ways. As Christians, we are priests in God's service, and we must guard against greed and offering our leftovers to God. God finds no pleasure in false or empty worship. It can be easy to use the New Covenant as an excuse not to tithe or be faithful in returning to God a portion in support of his church and mission in the world. Remember, where our treasure is there our hearts will be also. Christian giving supports God's cause to make his name great among the nations.

JONATHAN SOLE

THE WRITINGS

RUTH

Author:
The author is anonymous; Jewish tradition suggests Samuel, but that is debatable.

Date:
Ruth takes place during the time of the Judges (1380 – 1050 BC). The genealogy at the end suggests that it was written sometime during David's reign.

Theme:
God is kind and faithful to fulfill his covenant promises. He is also a redeemer of the Gentiles.

Summary:
Ruth begins in the days of the judges with a famine in Judah. Naomi's family travels to Moab, where one of her sons marries Ruth. Death strikes the family, and Naomi and Ruth move back to Judah. Ruth shows herself as kind and faithful and meets Boaz. Boaz cares for Ruth and eventually becomes her kinsman redeemer by marrying Ruth. This narrative account introduces the writings because it reminds readers of God's goodness and faithfulness. The genealogy at the end from Boaz to David shows that Seed of the Woman continues.

Key Passages:
In the days when the judges ruled there was a famine in the land, and a man of Bethlehem in Judah went to sojourn in the country of Moab (1:1).

But Boaz answered her, "All that you have done for your

mother-in-law since the death of your husband has been fully told to me, and how you left your father and mother and your native land and came to a people that you did not know before (2:11).

"May he be blessed by the LORD, whose kindness has not forsaken the living or the dead!...The man is a close relative of ours, one of our redeemers" (2:20).

And the women of the neighborhood gave him a name, saying, "A son has been born to Naomi." They named him Obed. He was the father of Jesse, the father of David" (4:17).

Christ Connection:
Jesus is the greater Boaz who redeems his people and saves them from sin and misery.

Application:
The story of Ruth speaks to how God redeems, not just through Boaz but even in the origin of the Moabites (see Gen 19:36-37). God is saving the foreigners and blesses the least likely. Believers should be encouraged to know that God rewards faithfulness. Although times seem harsh, remember, the faithful will shine. Set your gaze forward to the day when we hear, well done, good and faithful servant. God's story ends in blessing for his people. Continue living faithfully for the glory of God.

PSALMS

Author:
The Psalms have a collection of authors—Moses, David, Solomon, Asaph, The Sons of Korah, and Ethan the Ezahite.

Date:
The writing of specific Psalms dates from Moses to the return of exile. Ezra and the scribes likely finished the final form in Ezra's time (450 BC).

Theme:
The Psalms are a guide for private and corporate worship directed toward God. They also provide the words to pray no matter what the internal struggle is.

Summary:
The Psalms are a collection of five books that express human emotions from the depths of agony to the heights of rejoicing. The five books move from the reign of David (1&2) to the exile of Israel (3) and the restoration of Israel along with the reign of God (4&5). They teach how to relate to God in his word and through worship. The message is that Yahweh reigns, and his promise to send forth the King in whom all the peoples of the earth will be blessed is going to happen; therefore, let everything that has breath praise the LORD.

Key Passages:
Blessed is the man who walks not in the counsel of the wicked... but his delight is in the Law of the LORD, and on his Law he meditates day and night (1:1-2).

The Law of the LORD is perfect, reviving the soul; the testimony of the LORD is sure making wise the simple (19:7),

He who dwells in the shelter of the Most High will abide in the shadow of the Almighty. I will say to the LORD, "my refuge and my fortress, my God, in whom I trust" (91:1-2).

The stone that the builders rejected has become the cornerstone. This is the LORD's doing; it is marvelous in our eyes (118:22-23).

Christ Connection:
Jesus is the stone the builders rejected, the shepherd who leads his people beside still waters, and the King of Glory who ascends into heaven on his own merits. The connections to Jesus are too numerous to list them all.

Application:
The Psalms are for real life. We are to sing them, pray them, learn from them, and relate to them. The Psalms teach us what healthy and genuine expressions of emotions toward God look like. If you are struggling with your feelings, look to the Psalms. If you are wondering what appropriate expressions of worship look like, you will find them in the Psalms. Our worship of God comes from knowing his word and works, and the Psalms guide us. The conclusion of the Psalms is the conclusion of our lives: let everything that has breath praise the LORD.

JOB

Author:
The author of Job is unknown.

Date:
The date is unknown. Many scholars date it from 1800 – 500 B.C. The internal evidence is unclear but points to some time in the patriarchal period possibly between Genesis 11 and 12.

Theme:
Job addresses the problem of evil and how God allows suffering.

Summary:
Job offers an honest and raw view of suffering and its purposes in the world. Job is a good man, godly and blameless, yet tragedy strikes him. He loses everything from his family to his wealth and his health. His friends try to support him but offer lousy advice. The human tendency is to believe in retribution theology. Good things happen because of good actions and bad things happen because of wrong actions. The story of Job tells a different story, one in which God uses suffering to refine and grow his people. God comes to a broken Job at the end of Job, reveals Job's sinfulness, and ultimately blesses and restores his faithful servant.

Key Passages:
And the LORD said to Satan, "Have you considered my servant Job, that there is none like him on the earth, a blameless and upright man, who fears God and turns away from evil?" 9 Then

Satan answered the LORD and said, "Does Job fear God for no reason? (1:8–9).

"The LORD gave, and the LORD has taken away; blessed be the name of the LORD." Job did not sin or charge God with wrong (1:21-22).

"For I know that my Redeemer lives, and at the last he will stand upon the earth. And after my skin has been thus destroyed, yet in my flesh I shall see God" (19:25-26).

I know that you can do all things, and that no purpose of yours can be thwarted. Who is this that hides counsel without knowledge? Therefore I have uttered what I did not understand,
things too wonderful for me, which I did not know (42:2-3).

Christ Connection:
Jesus is the living redeemer whom all will see after death.

Application:
Job clearly shows us what is challenging in this life. Suffering happens, and we only sometimes know why. Job never gets told why, but to trust God. No matter life circumstances, remember that God is good, powerful, and knows what he is doing. Considering eternity, suffering is a light, momentary affliction. Remind yourself of that on those hard days. God cares. Also, be mindful of who your friends are. Be around those who support and build you up.

PROVERBS

Author:
King Solomon, the son of David, is the author. Agur and Lemuel received acknowledgment for the last two chapters.

Date:
Proverbs was written during the life of Solomon (970-931 BC) and complied during the reign of Hezekiah (729-686 BC).

Theme:
Proverbs is a book of practical wisdom that calls upon readers to follow God's direction.

Summary:
Proverbs is filled with ancient sayings that always remain relevant. Although contexts change over time, the path to true wisdom does not. Proverbs serves as a guide to living the life God intends for his people. The beginning of any understanding or actual knowledge is rooted in the fear of God. Proverbs consists of principles and practices to live by, not necessarily promises to claim. Wisdom and folly are enemies in the book, much like the Seed of the Woman and the Serpent. The blessed life is realized through heeding and applying the LORD's instruction.

Key Passages:
The fear of the LORD is the beginning of knowledge; fools despise wisdom and instruction (1:7).

Trust in the LORD with all your heart, and do not lean on your own understanding. In all your ways acknowledge him, and he will make straight your paths (3:6).

"Leave your simple ways, and live, and walk in the way of insight" (9:6).

Charm is deceitful, and beauty is vain, but a woman who fears the LORD is to be praised. Give her of the fruit of her hands, and let her works praise her in the gates (31:30-31).

Christ Connection:
Jesus is the wisdom of God made manifest. He embodies the most excellent way.

Application:
Proverbs is a book of application. This collection contains tips, pithy sayings, and proverbial realities for navigating life. In interpreting Proverbs, it is best to understand them as general rules of life and not exact promises to claim. Just because parents train their children in the LORD does not guarantee the child will continue in the faith, but there is a more substantial likelihood that it will happen. Go to Proverbs for how to manage money, deal with difficult people, and general wisdom. Proverbs gives us an example of the timelessness of the word of God. His message always continues to hit the mark in every generation. Make wisdom your pursuit in life, and do not neglect God's means of giving it.

ECCLESIASTES

Author:
Early Jewish and Christian traditions attribute authorship to Solomon. Although the author refers to himself as the Preacher, this leaves authorship uncertain.

Date:
Most scholars date the book between 970-930 BC.

Theme:
Ecclesiastes deals with the highs and lows of living in a world filled with sin and challenges.

Summary:
Ecclesiastes asks many of life's hard questions. At times, the writer seems to lament life "under the sun," and at other times, he seems to enjoy it. The Preacher asks many more questions than answers, pointing to human existence's complexity. However, the one constant throughout all of life is the lordship of God and how humans are to respond to him. While the Preacher gives instructions on living well, his conclusion provides a fitting summary for the book. The whole duty of man is to fear God and keep his commandments.

Key Passages:
Vanity of vanities, says the Preacher, vanity of vanities! All is vanity. What does man gain by all the toil at which he toils under the sun? (1:2-3).

For everything there is a season and a time for every matter under heaven: a time to be born, and a time to die (3:1-2).

Though a sinner does evil a hundred times and prolongs his life, yet I know that it will be well with those who fear God, because they fear before him (8:12).

The end of the matter; all has been heard. Fear God and keep his commandments, for this is the whole duty of man. For God will bring every deed into judgment, with every secret thing, whether good or evil (12:13-14).

Christ Connection:
Jesus is the meaning of life. Only through knowing him can one begin to see and understand the purpose of existence.

Application:
Ecclesiastes is refreshing because of its authentic author. In Christian circles, we often use cliché terminology and respond superficially to real problems. The reminder comes that life is complicated, confusing, and can appear quite frustrating at times. Yet, while things constantly change, God remains the same, and his requirements do not change. As followers of Jesus, we must enjoy the tasks we set out to do. Existence on earth is not simply a miserable time awaiting heaven. Let the redeemed of the Lord rejoice in God's creation and fulfill our duty, fearing God and keeping his commandments.

SONG OF SONGS

Author:
Solomon, the son of David, is either the author or the book's recipient.

Date:
Song of Songs was probably written sometime during the life of Solomon (10th century BC).

Theme:
Song of Songs describes a relationship beinging with courtship leading to marriage and the various stages couples go through.

Summary:
Song of Songs magnifies the beauty of human love between a man and a woman. Love and intimacy are gifts from God and a blessing to spouses. The book is a series of love poems that traces the progress of a relationship from initial attraction to maturity. The vivid language expresses the special bond of intimacy within the confines of marriage. The author gives warnings about seeking pleasure outside the marriage relationship. God designed marriage for enjoyment, viewed as positive, and a continual pursuit of one another throughout the years. Marital love is fierce, powerful, and sacrificial.

Key Passages:
I adjure you, O daughters of Jerusalem, by the gazelles or the does of the field, that you not stir up or awaken love until it pleases (2:7).

I am my beloved's and my beloved is mine; he grazes among the lilies (6:3).

Set me as a seal upon your heart, as a seal upon your arm, for love is strong as death, jealousy is fierce as the grave. Its flashes are flashes of fire, the very flame of the LORD. Many waters cannot quench love, neither can floods drown it. If a man offered for love all the wealth of his house, he would be utterly despised (8:6-7).

Christ Connection:
Jesus' love for his bride, the church, is illustrated through the expression in Song of Songs. The book is not an allegory of Jesus and the church, however.

Application:
Marriage is designed for enjoyment, physical intimacy, and lifelong love. God created intimacy for enjoyment within the boundaries of marriage. For the married, read Song of Songs with your spouse and talk through the experience. Some of the compliments were culturally bound to Israel in the 10th century, but the spirit and tone behind them are worthy of consideration. To the unmarried, do not practice behavior God has restricted to the marriage relationship. When we operate according to God's wise plan, we will enjoy the blessings of the good life. Marriage is God's gift to humanity and must be cherished and nurtured till the end.

LAMENTATIONS

Author:
The author is anonymous, but historical tradition believes that Jeremiah, the weeping prophet, is the author.

Date:
Lamentations was written shortly after the destruction of Jerusalem in 586 BC.

Theme:
Lamentations express grief and mourning over sin and judgment, but God is faithful in suffering.

Summary:
Lamentations is a series of five laments that express the loss of Jerusalem and Israel as a nation. The first lament focuses on the destruction of Jerusalem. The second lament considers the country in exile. The third lament is personal from the author and gives a picture of his struggle but also of hope. God's steadfast love never ceases. The fourth lament focuses on the suffering of those who survived the destruction of Jerusalem. The fifth lament is a cry from the people that the LORD would restore them. They fear rejection and that the LORD has abandoned them because of their covenant breaking.

Key Passages:
Judah has gone into exile because of affliction and hard servitude: she dwells now among the nations, but finds no resting place; her pursuers have all overtaken her in the midst of her distress" (1:3).

"Arise, cry out in the night, at the beginning of the night watches! Pour out your heart like water before the presence of the LORD! Lift your hands to him for the lives of your children, who faint for hunger at the head of every street (2:19).

But this I call to mind, and therefore I have hope: The steadfast love of the LORD never ceases; his mercies never come to an end; they are new every morning; great is your faithfulness (3:21-23).

Restore us to yourself, O LORD, that we may be restored! Renew our days as of old (5:21).

Christ Connection:
Lamentations find fulfillment in Jesus, who reconciles believers to God and appeased the Father's wrath. Jesus too weeps over the state of Jerusalem.

Application:
God will deliver what he promises. For Israel, this was a blessing for obedience and a curse for disobedience. Although God punished Israel for disobedience, the message of Lamentations is hope in suffering. God's steadfast love never ceases, and as followers of Jesus, we must remember that God loves even in our suffering. Make Lam. 3:21-23 your morning prayer during deep grief and soul pain. No one can separate us from the love of God in Christ Jesus our Lord.

DANIEL

Author:
Scholars believe Daniel has written significant portions of the book that bear his name, if not all.

Date:
The book begins in 605 BC and concludes in the mid 530's BC. Daniel spans 70 years.

Theme:
God is the ultimate sovereign, even when the wicked prosper.

Summary:
Nebuchadnezzar has destroyed Israel and taken God's people in exile. Cyrus, the king of Persia, conquers Babylon and sends a wave of exiles back to Jerusalem. Ultimately, though, it is the LORD who is in control. Daniel conveys faith, hope, and perseverance during unsettling times. Structurally, Daniel is a historical narrative (1-6) and then apocalyptic prophecies (7-12). Daniel demonstrates consistency in his faithfulness to the LORD in a foreign land. Popular accounts are the refusing to eat the king's food, the fiery furnace, and the lion's den. Dainel's vision of the Son of Man standing before the Ancient of Days is central to the prophetic portion.

Key Passages:
And God gave Daniel favor and compassion in the sight of the chief of the eunuchs (1:9).

"Our God whom we serve is able to deliver us from the burning *fiery furnace...But if not, be it is known to you, O king, that we will not serve your gods or worship the golden image that you have set up" (3:17-18).*

"For his dominion is an everlasting dominion, and his kingdom endures from generation to generation" (4:34b).

"There came one like a son of man, and he came to the Ancient of Days and was presented before him. And to him was given dominion and glory and a kingdom, that all peoples, nations, and languages should serve him" (7:13-14).

Christ Connection:
Jesus is the Son of Man who stands before the Ancient of Days and has received all authority in heaven and on earth. He is the stone that was cut out of the mountain that crushed the nations and filled the earth.

Application:
Daniel calls upon us to remain faithful amid opposition. No matter how powerful the opposition is, our God rules and reigns. We truly start living for Jesus when we have come to the point of surrendering our lives, even if called upon to die. Many speculate about Daniel's prophecies and fulfillment. Jesus fulfills Daniel's visions by ushering in the great and final kingdom. Christian, stand firm and be courageous; you belong to Victor's kingdom. Rejoice; the Lord is King. You can overcome any opposition because greater is he that is in you than he that is in the world.

ESTHER

Author:
The author is unknown; some scholars believe Mordecai could be the author.

Date:
The unknown author wrote sometime near the end of King Ahasuerus' reign (460-430 BC).

Theme:
God is sovereign, and his providential care is visible even when he is not.

Summary:
Although Esther does not mention God's name, a careful reading shows his hand orchestrating the events. Esther has providentially remained in Persia after the release of exiles back to Jerusalem. When she became queen of Persia, God raised her for such a time as this. Haman plots to eradicate the Jews, but Esther, through Mordecai, reveals Haman's plot to the king. She risked her own life for the salvation of her people, and as a result, God's people received rescue. A significant reversal occurs, and Haman dies while Mordecai is honored. The victory of the Jews celebrates God's sovereign care for his covenant people.

Key Passages:
Esther had not made known her people or kindred, for Mordecai had commanded her not to make it known (2:10).

"For if you keep silent at this time, relief and deliverance will rise for the Jews from another place, but you and your father's

house will perish. And who knows whether you have not come to the kingdom for such a time as this?" (4:14).

"I and my young women will also fast as you do. Then I will go to the king, though it is against the Law, and if I perish, I perish (4:16).

"If Mordecai, before whom you have begun to fall, is of the Jewish people, you will not overcome him but will surely fall before him" (6:13).

Christ Connection:
Jesus, like Esther, became the mediator to rescue his people.

Application:
Esther tells the story of God's mysterious providence in working out his people's salvation. We will face times when we struggle in faith and do not feel or see God at work, but rest assured he is. God sent forth his Son so that we might experience the fullness of his grace in Christ. Just because we cannot see him, we know he is there, and he is the sovereign protector of his people. Also, know that God may be raising you up for such a time as this. Ultimately, sleep well at night; God is in control.

EZRA

Author:
Ezra, the priest-scribe, wrote the book that bears his name.

Date:
Ezra dates from the middle to the close of the 5th century B.C. (460-420 BC).

Theme:
God is faithful in his covenant relationship with his people, and the human heart needs to change.

Summary:
Ezra tells the story of the return of the Jews from exile and the rebuilding of Jerusalem. The events described in the book span roughly 100 years. The return to Jerusalem was with struggle. Many Jews were born during the exile and lived under the judgment of God in a foreign land. Once they were permitted to return, they began to rebuild the temple, and after many obstacles, they completed the 2nd temple. Despite the new temple, Ezra finds ongoing sinfulness among the people when he arrives. A new temple would not bring about lasting change; they needed a new heart.

Key Passages:
And this house was finished on the third day of the month of Adar, in the sixth year of the reign of Darius the King (6:15).

For Ezra had set his heart to study the Law of the LORD and to do it and teach his statutes and rules in Israel (7:10).

"The hand of our God is for good on all who seek him, and the power of his wrath is against all who forsake him" (8:22).

"Now then make confession to the LORD, the God of your fathers and do his will. Separate yourselves from the peoples of the land and from the foreign wives" (10:11).

Christ Connection:
Through Jesus comes a final return from exile into everlasting fellowship with God in the eternal promised land.

Application:
God is not forgetful but remains faithful in his covenant love. Ezra prepares us for the cost of faithfulness. Opposition will come our way when we step out in faith and obedience. Following Jesus is costly but extremely rewarding. Furthermore, Ezra models how we approach God's word: study, apply, and teach it. Growth in Christlikeness comes through constant intentional exposure to his word. Following Jesus means our task is to make disciples, and as we study, apply, and teach God's word, we are accomplishing the task Jesus has given us. The final part of Ezra is a warning. Complacency breeds sin. The returned exiles fell into the same patterns that got their ancestors exiled. We must guard against complacency and falling into subtle sins that begin to pile up. Through the word and prayer, we can remain faithful these days.

NEHEMIAH

Author:
Although the author is anonymous, Nehemiah contributed large portions of the book, and Jewish tradition considers Ezra the author.

Date:
Nehemiah overlaps with Ezra from 445 - 424 BC.

Theme:
Nehemiah shows that the marks of godly leadership are conviction and courage amid opposition.

Summary:
Nehemiah goes out with the third wave of exiles and settles back in Jerusalem and serves as the governor. The issue this time is that the city is defenseless and needs the walls repaired. Nehemiah set his heart to do what God gave him, and he persevered through internal disunity and opposition from others. In the end, Nehemiah successfully sees that the walls of Jerusalem are completed. Now, with a rebuilt temple and walls, Nehemiah has Ezra read from the Law and calls upon them to be faithful to the words of Moses. Reading the Law leads to a time of corporate confession and covenant renewal.

Key Passages:
"The remnant there in the province who had survived the exile is in great trouble and shame. The wall of Jerusalem is broken down, and its gates are destroyed by fire" (1:3).

So the wall was finished on the twenty-fifth day of the month

Elul, in fifty-two days. And when all our enemies heard of it, all the nations around us were afraid and fell greatly in their own esteem, for they perceived that this work had been accomplished with the help of our God (6:15-16).

They read from the book, the Law of God, clearly and gave the sense so that the people understood the reading (8:8).

"And do not be grieved, for the joy of the LORD is your strength" (8:10b).

Christ Connection:
What sin has broken, Jesus rebuilds. Through his finished work on the cross, he restores people to God.

Application:
Nehemiah shows us what godly leadership looks like. Prayer precedes action, action is fueled by conviction, and conviction allows a leader to stand courageously in opposition. Leading is hard, but if God has placed you in that role, you should commit to being a person of conviction and courage. Do not allow opposition to halt you in what God has placed upon your heart. Stand firm, be bold, remain faithful, follow Jesus, and seek to accomplish great things for God. Godly leadership only happens through intentional effort and understanding.

1&2 CHRONICLES

Author:
The author's identity is unknown. Jewish tradition considers Ezra the author, but the evidence is inconclusive.

Date:
Chronicles was likely written sometime after the first wave of exiles until Ezra (538-450 BC).

Theme:
Chronicles is an essentially optimistic book retelling the history of Israel and looking for future hope.

Summary:
The 1st and 2nd Chronicles were one book until the Greek translation. They retell the history of Israel through genealogy, with a primary focus on David and the Southern Kingdom of Judah. The English Bible places Chronicles after Kings, which can seem confusing or redundant to the reader. Kings focuses on the reign of the Kings while Chronicles is focused on the temple and worship. Chronicles begins with Adam and ends with the return from exile; it is best to see this book as the close of the O.T. It is a message of hope that God is faithful and the Seed of the Woman, the Offspring of Abraham, from the tribe of Judah, the Son of David, will rule and reign.

Key Passages:
"When your days are fulfilled to walk with your fathers, I will raise up your offspring after you, one of your own sons, and I will establish his kingdom. He shall build a house for me, and I will establish his throne forever" (1 Chron. 17:11-12).

"Be strong and courageous and do it. Do not be afraid and do not be dismayed, for the LORD God, even my God, is with you. He will not leave you or forsake you, until all the work for the service of the house of the LORD is finished (1 Chron. 28:20).

"O LORD, God of Israel, there is no God like you, in heaven or on earth, keeping covenant and showing steadfast love to your servants who walk before you with all their heart (2 Chron. 6:14).

Christ Connection:
Jesus is the Son of David who comes to restore, renew, and reconcile people to God.

Application:
Genesis begins with God's people in a promised land and going into exile. Chronicles ends with God's people coming out of exile and back into the promised land. The message is one of hope and restoration. Sin will not have the final word, for God is a redeemer. As the curtain of the O.T. closes, there is a cautious optimism with a look to the future Son of David, a Messiah who will rule and reign. Though times seem harsh, God is working in and through you for his glory and your good. Rejoice that Chronicles is not the last word; we are not awaiting a Messiah; we have Jesus and await his return and the permanent promised land.

THE NEW TESTAMENT

Four hundred years have passed since the last inspired writing. The Scriptures of the New Testament were all written in the first century AD. The books tell the story of Jesus the Messiah, from his birth, ministry, death, and resurrection to the aftermath of the Christ event. While the NT only makes up twenty-five percent of the Bible, Christians prioritize it over the OT. This means the OT provides information for the NT, and the NT is the interpretative key to understanding the OT.

The NT has 27 books in a variety of genres. The Gospels are their genre, close to ancient biographies but not wholly. Acts is a historical narrative. Romans through Jude are epistles/letters. Hebrews is likely a transcribed sermon/letter that did circulate. Revelation is an apocalyptic letter to seven churches. The first record of the 27 books in the current English order comes from a tract Athanasius penned on Christmas Day 365 AD.

Revelation serves not only as the end of the N.T. but also as the fitting final book of the Bible. Man and woman began in God's paradise, living in fellowship with him. Ultimately, God's people will be in paradise, living in fellowship with him. Just this time, it is permanent because sin is defeated, and the grace of God has perfected the followers of Jesus Christ through the person and work of his Son. The story in Scripture is that the King slays the dragon and saves his bride. God wins.

THE GOSPELS AND ACTS

MATTHEW

Author:
Although the writer never mentions his name, the church has long recognized the apostle Matthew as the sole author.

Date:
Matthew was likely written in the 50s or early 60s.

Theme:
Jesus is the Messiah who fulfills the OT prophecies.

Summary:
Matthew wrote to convince his Jewish readers of the messiahship of Jesus of Nazareth. Matthew picks up where Chronicles ends and serves as a bridge into the New Testament. The use of genealogy to begin the gospels connects Jesus to the lineage of David and the promise made to Abraham. The genealogy of Jesus is the final one in all the scripture because he is the fulfillment of all God's promises. Matthew structures his gospel with five major discourses the Jewish reader saw as a connection to the five books of Moses—Jesus' authority as king and sovereign rule run as a thread throughout the account. Matthew's Sermon on the Mount is Jesus' most extended continuous recorded discourse. The conclusion is the great commission to make disciples.

Key Passages:
The book of the genealogy of Jesus Christ, the son of David, the Son of Abraham" (1:1).

"She will bear a son, and you shall call his name Jesus, for he

will save his people from their sins" (1:21)

And when Jesus finished these sayings, the crowds were astonished at his teaching, for he was teaching them as one who had authority, and not as their scribes (7:28-29).

"All authority in heaven and on earth has been given to me. Go therefore and make disciples of all nations, baptizing them in the name of the Father, and of the Son, and of the Holy Spirit, teaching them to observe all that I have commanded you. And behold, I am with you always, to the end of the age (28:18-20).

Christ Connection:
Jesus is God's anointed who possesses all authority in heaven and on earth.

Application:
Matthew teaches us that Jesus fulfills the Old Testament promises. We are not looking for another, nor can we improve upon what Jesus taught and did. Let us make obedience to Jesus our number one priority. Following Jesus is our created purpose, and it unites us back to the Father through the redemption accomplished by the Son and applied by the Spirit. We must take discipleship seriously because Jesus commanded and commissioned his followers to do it.

MARK

Author:
Like Matthew, the author does not name himself. Church tradition has always credited John Mark as the author.

Date:
Mark was probably the first gospel written, based much on Peter's preaching in the 50s.

Theme:
Jesus is the Son of God, who has power over demons, diseases, and death.

Summary:
Mark is an action-packed narrative that shifts scenes quickly. He wrote to bring his predominantly gentile Roman audience face-to-face with Jesus as swiftly as possible. Jesus is depicted as the one recognized as divine by the demons but primarily misunderstood by everyone else. The religious leaders hate him, the disciples struggle to understand him, and the crowds use him. Ultimately, Mark shows his readers that Jesus is the divine son of God who crushed the head of the serpent through his death and resurrection. Miracles and the spiritual world make up a large part of the first half of the gospel, while the second half is about going to Jerusalem and eventually suffering crucifixion.

Key Passages:
And whenever the unclean spirits saw him, they fell down before him and cried out, "You are the Son of God" (3:11).

And they were filled with great fear and said to one another, "Who then is this, that even the wind and the sea obey him?" (4:41).

And he asked them, "But who do you say that I am?" Peter answered him, "You are the Christ" (8:29).

"Are you the Christ, the Son of the Blessed? And Jesus said, I am, and you will see the Son of Man seated at the right hand of Power, and coming with the clouds of heaven (14:61-62).

Christ Connection:
Jesus is displayed as the divine Son of God who ushers in the kingdom of God through his life, death, and resurrection. His miracles and teachings testify to his identity.

Application:
Mark brings his readers face-to-face with Jesus early and often. He forces us to ask and answer the question of who Jesus is. This book is excellent for discipling a new believer or someone interested in learning more about Jesus. We can rely on Jesus' salvation, accomplished through the cross, because of who he is: the divine Son of God. Let your heart be transformed as you dive into Mark's action-packed narrative and immediately encounter Jesus, the Son of Man, the Son of God.

LUKE

Author:
Although the book does not mention the author's name, all evidence points to Luke, Paul's companion, as the author.

Date:
Luke was written sometime in the early 60's.

Theme:
Luke writes so his readers know Jesus came to seek and save the lost, outcast, and oppressed.

Summary:
Luke writes to present the undeniable reality that Jesus of Nazareth has turned the world upside down. He wants his readers to know with certainty what they have been taught through oral tradition. Luke gives the most detailed account of Jesus's miraculous birth and some famous parables. One of Luke's unique contributions to the story of Jesus is the emphasis on Jesus' love for the outcast. Written as a gentile, he writes to prepare the reader for the mass influx of Gentiles who will trust in Jesus the Messiah in the book of Acts. He concludes his narrative by sharing the account where Jesus explained everything that happened to him through the Old Testament.

Key Passages:
It seemed good to me, also, having followed all things closely for some time past, to write an orderly account for you, most excellent Theophilus, that you may have certainty concerning the things you have been taught (1:3-4).

He said to him, "If they do not hear Moses and the Prophets, neither will they be convinced if someone should rise from the dead (16:31).

And Jesus said to him, "Today salvation has come to this house, since he also is a son of Abraham. For the Son of came to seek and to save the lost" (19:9-10).

"These are my words that I spoke to you while I was still with you, that everything written about me in the Law of Moses and the Prophets and the Psalms must be fulfilled. Then he opened their minds to understand the Scriptures (24:44-45).

Christ Connection:
Jesus is the pursuer of sinners and delights in their salvation.

Application:
Luke writes very much like an educated historian. We are overwhelmed with Jesus' compassion for the least of these and the outcast. Luke shows us that no one is too far gone to receive the grace of the Lord Jesus. Never give up hope for the lost people in your life. Keep on praying, for Jesus came to save the lost. We will rejoice with all of heaven when one sinner repents. Ask the Lord to give you an excitement for the salvation of those who come to Christ. Luke also gives us a key to understanding that every book of the Bible has a connection with Christ. The Scriptures are fulfilled in Jesus.

JOHN

Author:
Like the other gospels, the author is anonymous. The traditional understanding is that John, the son of Zebedee, wrote it.

Date:
John was likely written sometime after the temple's destruction between 70-90 A.D.

Theme:
Jesus is the Messiah, the Son of God who provides eternal life.

Summary:
While the first three gospel writers have significant overlap in their material, the Gospel of John is unique in much of its material. John is written for evangelistic purposes for a well-educated Jewish audience in O.T. themes and messianic expectations. The theology is rich and deep. John provides seven signs that display Jesus' divinity and highlight Jesus' call to saving faith in him. The sovereignty of God is the salvation of sinners, which receives great attention. John provides his purpose statement near the end of the gospel, and it consists of knowing, believing, and trusting in Jesus of Nazareth as the Messiah, the Son of God, the One who secured eternal life for all who believe.

Key Passages:
"And the Word became flesh and dwelt among us, and we have seen his glory, glory as of the only Son from the Father, full of grace and truth" (1:14).

"For God so loved the world, that he gave his only Son, that whoever believes in him should not perish but have eternal life" (3:16).

"You search the Scriptures because you think that in them you have eternal life; and it is they that bear witness about me, yet you refuse to come to me that you may have life" (5:39-40).

Jesus said to him, "I am the way, and the truth, and the life. No one comes to the Father except through me" (14:6)

Christ Connection:

Jesus is the eternally existent 2nd member of the Trinity who became man to bring man back to God.

Application:

John seeks to convince his readers that Jesus is the sole source of salvation. Jesus is the author of life and the meaning of life, and through his death and resurrection, he secured eternal life for all who believe. Jesus' work on your behalf is sufficient in this life and the life to come. The challenge for many is resting in the reality that Jesus accomplished everything needed for our salvation. John calls on all to trust in Jesus alone; nothing can be added or subtracted from Jesus' work. The Son of God gave his life for you; if you trust him, you are secure in him.

ACTS

Author:
Luke is the author of Acts and the gospel that bears his name.

Date:
Luke wrote Acts sometime in the early 60's AD.

Theme:
Acts traces the aftermath of Jesus' resurrection and the explosive growth of the 1st-century church through the apostolic witness.

Summary:
Acts picks up with Jesus' final words, commissioning his disciples to bear witness to the resurrection. Luke follows the growth of the church from Jerusalem to Judea, Samaria, and the ends of the earth. The ministry of Peter makes up a large portion of the book's first half—the second half documents Paul's apostolic ministry. The supernatural work of the Holy Spirit empowering preaching, giving boldness, converting people, and exalting Jesus runs throughout the book. Acts introduces a significant paradigm shift in understanding who the people of God are. Jews and Gentiles receive equal standing and come together to comprise the church of Jesus Christ. Acts concludes with the Gospel reaching Rome and Paul under house arrest.

Key Passages:
"But you will receive power when the Holy Spirit has come upon you, and you will be my witnesses in Jerusalem and in all Judea

and Samaria, and to the end of the earth" (1:8).

And they devoted themselves to the apostles' teaching and the fellowship, to the breaking of bread and the prayers. And awe came upon every soul, and many wonders and signs were being done through the apostles (2:42-43).

"But we believe that we will be saved through the grace of the Lord Jesus, just as they will" (15:11).

"These men who have turned the world upside down have come here also" (17:6).

Christ Connection:
Jesus is the ascended Lord through whom salvation is proclaimed and received.

Application:
Acts tells the story of how the church exploded onto the scene. Jesus promised to build his church, which is observed in Acts through the empowerment of the Holy Spirit. Today, the local church is a continual sign of Jesus' plan and mission. The power of the gospel will prevail, and it is lived out in and through the community of the people of God. Love your church, love the people in your church, love the Head of the church, and give yourself to the church's mission: pleasing God and making disciples of Jesus Christ.

JONATHAN SOLE

THE LETTERS OF PAUL

ROMANS

Author:
The Apostle Paul wrote Romans.

Date:
Romans was written around 57 AD.

Theme:
Romans explains how the gospel is the power of God unto salvation for everyone who believes.

Summary:
Romans is Paul's letter to the church in Rome, which he had yet to meet. One of his reasons for writing is to secure a partnership with the church to bring the gospel to Spain. Romans is Paul's most systematic explanation of God's plan of salvation to include Jews and Gentiles. Structurally, Romans can be divided into two major sections. Chapters 1-11 are steeped in theological reasoning, and 12-16 is the application of theology in actions and attitudes. In chapters 1-3, Paul establishes that all humankind has sinned and deserves God's justice equally. Jesus satisfies divine justice, and chapters 4 and 5 demonstrate that believers are declared righteous by faith in Jesus. Chapters 6-8 deal with living out justification through progressive sanctification. In chapters 9-11, Paul wrestles with God's election, Israel's rejection, and God's plan to unite his people as the church. The remainder of the book deals with believers' relationships to God, one another, and authorities.

Key Passages:
For I am not ashamed of the gospel, for it is the power of God

for salvation to everyone who believes, to the Jew first and also to the Greek (1:16).

"None is righteous, no, not one" (3:10).

And we know that for those who love God all things work together for good, for those who are called according to his purpose (8:28).

I appeal to you therefore, brothers, by the mercies of God, to present your bodies as a living sacrifice, holy and acceptable to God, which is your spiritual worship. Do not be conformed to this world, but be transformed by the renewal of your mind (12:1-2).

Christ Connection:
Jesus is the justifier of the ungodly and has secured eternal redemption for all who have faith in him.

Application:
Romans speaks hope amid challenging times. God's love for us, demonstrated in the death of Christ, is unbreakable, and we can never be separated from it. Romans has a good word for your soul wherever you are in your Christian journey. The book's structure teaches us that the truth of what God has done for us in Christ propels our love, service, and relationships to God and others. No matter the circumstance, remember that God has set his everlasting love upon you for his glory and your good. Trust his goodness. Remember, truth understood is truth loved and truth lived.

1 CORINTHIANS

Author:
Paul wrote the letter to the Corinthians.

Date:
Paul wrote the letter while in Ephesus around 55 AD.

Theme:
First Corinthians is a letter of correction to a worldly and divided church.

Summary:
First Corinthians is an example of what not to be as a church. Paul opens his letter by appealing to them to be united in Christ and not divided by which preacher they follow. Later, Paul addresses a situation where the Corinthians ignored sexual immorality in the church. The fundamental issue is that the Corinthian church was not much different than the Corinthian culture. The culture celebrated sexual promiscuity, religious diversity, female authority, and selfish agendas. Paul urges the church to pursue holiness, the glory of God, love, and healthy masculinity. He concludes his letter by teaching the gospel and the hope of resurrection, highlighting that the dead will rise one day and put on immortality.

Key Passages:
And because of him you are in Christ Jesus, who became to us wisdom from God, righteousness and sanctification and redemption so that, as it is written, "Let the one who boasts, boast in the Lord" (1:30-31).

So, whether you eat or drink, or whatever you do, do all to the glory of God (10:31).

Love is patient and kind; love does not envy or boast it is not arrogant or rude. It does not insist on its own way; it is not irritable or resentful; it does not rejoice at wrongdoing, but rejoices with the truth. Love bears all things, believes all things, hopes all things, endures all things. Love never ends (13:4-8).

Be steadfast, immovable, always abounding in the work of the Lord, knowing that in the Lord your labor is not in vain (15:58).

Christ Connection:
Jesus is the uniter of those who are saved because he is the wisdom, righteousness, sanctification, and redemption needed.

Application:
1 Corinthians is written culturally; therefore, Paul addresses specific issues. Principally, 1 Corinthians reminds us of our call to be separate from the ungodly culture around us. The church needs to help shape the culture and not be shaped by it. Do not compromise to cultural pressure, remain steadfast, cling to your brothers and sisters in Christ, and let all you do be done in love. Our lives are a witness to the world of Jesus. When the church mixes itself with the world in an attempt to be culturally relevant the slow demise begins. Compromise begins when we look outside the Word of God for acceptable practices and behaviors in the church.

2 CORINTHIANS

Author:
Paul wrote 2 Corinthians.

Date:
Paul wrote the letter around 56 AD, roughly a year after 1 Corinthians.

Theme:
Paul defends his ministry and calls upon the believers to be unified with him.

Summary:
Second Corinthians addresses some previous issues addressed in 1 Corinthians, namely the restoration of the man the church disciplined. In chapters 3-6, Paul highlights the reality of gospel ministry and its cost. In the middle of the letter, he gives instructions on giving and then turns to defend his ministry against the accusations of self-proclaimed apostles. Paul emphasizes that suffering as an apostle is a sign of authenticity, and he boasts of his weakness, not strength. He concludes with a final warning to the Corinthians to accept his genuine ministry, examine themselves, and live in peace among each other.

Key Passages:
Blessed be the God and Father of our Lord Jesus Christ, the Father of mercies and God of all comfort, who comforts us in all our affliction, so that we may be able to comfort those who are in any affliction, with the comfort with which we ourselves are comforted by God (1:3-4).

For our sake he made him to be sin who knew no sin, so that in him we might become the righteousness of God (5:21).

For godly grief produces a repentance that leads to salvation without regret, whereas worldly grief produces death (7:10).

For the weapons of our warfare are not of the flesh but have divine power to destroy strongholds (10:4).

Christ Connection:
Although Jesus never sinned, the Father made him to be sin so that all who trust in him will be treated as the most righteous saints.

Application:
Serving for the kingdom of God is both costly and rewarding. Not every day is happy in Jesus, but God does supply grace and joy for the journey. Hard days, long nights, and suffering await anyone who desires to follow Jesus' call to make disciples. Good things are not easy in life; the best things take effort to overcome challenges and opposition. The greatest thing we can do in this life is serve God by laboring to make disciples of Jesus Christ. When hardship comes your way, embrace the hard and look beyond to what is eternal. Since we have this ministry by the mercy of God, we do not lose heart. Give yourself for something greater than yourself.

GALATIANS

Author:
Paul wrote the letter to the Galatians.

Date:
Galatians is probably Paul's first letter, written sometime around 50 AD.

Theme:
Galatians is a fiery letter intended to expose and combat legalism.

Summary:
Galatians addresses the timeless issue of legalism. The churches in Galatia had fallen into the trap of adding to the gospel. The specific matter is that people were teaching that Christians needed to receive the sign of the old covenant to be accepted by God. Paul rightly understood that circumcision was an outward work, and God accepts Christians solely upon the merits of Jesus, not the works of the law. Paul's central message is justification by faith and not by works. The result of justification is the fruit-bearing life in the Spirit. Paul concludes with an exhortation to bear one another's burdens and a potent reminder that new life matters most, not external conformity.

Key Passages:
But even if we or an angel from heaven should preach to you a gospel contrary to the one we preached to you, let him be accursed (1:8).

I have been crucified with Christ. It is no longer I who live, but

Christ who lives in me. And the life I now live in the flesh I live by faith in the Son of God, who loved me and gave himself for me (2:20).

Christ redeemed us from the curse of the law by becoming a curse for us, for it is written, "Cursed is everyone who is hanged on a tree" (3:14).

But the fruit of the Spirit is love, joy, peace, patience, kindness, goodness, faithfulness, gentleness, self control; against such things there is no law (5:22).

Christ Connection:
Jesus was cursed in his crucifixion to bless all who believe in him.

Application:
Legalism is not an error of Christianity but another gospel. If we add any work beyond the finished work of Jesus, it pollutes the gospel and changes the message. Salvation is by grace alone through faith alone in Christ alone. Faith equals salvation that results in good works. If you struggle to wonder if God is pleased with your performance, you must look to Jesus. God is glad in us because he is pleased in the perfect obedience to Jesus. Refuse the temptation to add requirements for salvation that the gospel does not. Faith in Christ will result in the fruit-bearing life in the Spirit. Trust in him alone. Faith and repentance is what the gospel requires. Obedience is what the gospel produces.

EPHESIANS

Author:
The apostle Paul wrote the letter to the Ephesians.

Date:
Ephesians was written while Paul was in prison, sometime around 60-62 AD.

Theme:
Paul writes to show God's glory in his plan for the church through the work of Jesus Christ.

Summary:
Ephesians begins with the profound truth that God has selected and elected a people through Jesus Christ. Based solely upon the character of God, he has taken the spiritual dead and given new life in Christ. Through Christ, there is one chosen people of God, the church. After Paul establishes the theological foundation for Christian beliefs, he moves to Christian behavior. In the first three chapters, Paul gives one command. The final three chapters are filled with the imperatives of the Christian life. Paul focuses on living out God's grace in the church, individual relationships, marriage and family, and the workplace. Paul concludes with the emphatic command to stand firm by putting on God's armor.

Key Passages:
Even as he chose us in him before the foundation of the world, that we should be holy and blameless before him (1:4).

For by grace you have been saved through faith. And this is not your own doing; it is the gift of God, not a result of works, so that no one may boast (2:8-9).

And he gave the apostles, the prophets, the evangelists, the shepherds and teachers, to equip the saints for the work of the ministry, for building up the body of Christ (4:11-12).

Therefore take up the whole armor of God, that you may be able to withstand in the evil day, and having done all, to stand firm (6:13).

Christ Connection:
Jesus is the head of the church as well as the cornerstone. His reconciliation unites God and man and brings unity to the church.

Application:
Ephesians shows us the importance of correct theology. Christianity is about knowing before doing. The truth of who we are in Christ fuels the Christian ethic. God has eternally blessed you by forgiving, loving, and giving you the inheritance Christ secured through his death and resurrection. We can live in unity and peace with one another because we share in the same Jesus. Remember, the gospel motivates behavior. Put off what is sinful and put on what is holy because God has chosen you and is conforming you to the likeness of Jesus. Be sure to stand firm and stand with your fellow brothers and sisters. As we put on the armor of God we can stand together as the church of God. Our strength comes as we remain close to Christ and the community of believers he produces.

PHILIPPIANS

Author:
Paul identifies himself as the author of the letter.

Date:
Philippians is one of the prison letters written in Rome around 60 AD.

Theme:
Philippians highlights joy, unity, and contentment in Christ.

Summary:
Paul writes to express his thankfulness to the believers in Philippi. He begins with a heartfelt prayer of joy and updates the gospel's advancement despite his imprisonment. He calls the Philippians to complete his joy by sharing in the mind of Christ; specifically, he calls for humility to manifest in unity. Jesus serves as the supreme display of this by humbling himself to the point of death. Paul expresses his love for Christ and reliance on Jesus' righteousness through his testimony and calls them to press on and look forward to the upward call of God. After a final appeal to unity, the focus shifts to divine contentment, with Paul sharing his secret that he can do all things through Christ, who strengthens him.

Key Passages:
And I am sure of this, that he who began a good work in you will bring it to completion at the day of Jesus Christ (1:6).

At the name of Jesus every knee should bow, in heaven and on earth and under the earth, and every tongue confess that Jesus Christ is Lord, to the glory of God the Father (2:10-11).

Indeed, I count everything as loss because of the surpassing worth of knowing Christ Jesus my Lord (3:8).

I know how to be brought low, and I know how to abound. In any and every circumstance, I have learned the secret of facing plenty and hunger, abundance and need. I can do all things through him who strengthens me (4:12-13).

Christ Connection:
Jesus demonstrated the supreme form of humility by taking on the form of a servant and laying down his life on the cross. He is the source of the believer's contentment and the fountain from which true joy flows.

Application:
Philippians reminds us that the gospel produces peace, humility, and unity. Whenever we disagree, they do not have to turn into disunity. Christ's example of humility needs to be where we constantly return when facing challenging relationships or difficult people. A gospel-centered life is also manifested in contentment. We live in a world today that is everything but content. As followers of Jesus, we have an incredible opportunity to display how the gospel satisfies and produces contentment despite our circumstances. If you struggle with joy, unity, or contentment, go to Philippians and pray that these words become a reality. We can do all things through him who strengthens us.

COLOSSIANS

Author:
Paul wrote to the church in Colossae.

Date:
Paul wrote to the Colossians while in prison, and at the same time, he wrote Ephesians 60-62 AD.

Theme:
Colossians focuses on the supremacy of Jesus and how the church should conduct itself.

Summary:
Like all the letters, Colossians addresses a specific issue in the church. There was some form of angel worship, recognizing special days, and legalism that plagued the church. Paul writes to clear the distractions of heresy and point the Colossians to the majesty of Jesus. Paul clearly states that Jesus is the image of the invisible God, and all the fullness of God dwells in him. He alone is the object of worship and praise. Since Christians have been united to Jesus, they are to put on the new self and put to death the remaining sin. Paul gives general instructions for Christians living with one another, in the household, and toward those not in the faith community.

Key Passages:
He is the image of the invisible God, the firstborn of all creation. For by him all things were created, in heaven and on earth, visible and invisible, whether thrones or dominions or rulers or authorities all things were created through him and for him (1:15-16).

Him we proclaim, warning everyone and teaching everyone with all wisdom, that we may present everyone mature in Christ (1:28).

Set your mind on things that are above, not on things that are on earth (3:2).

And whatever you do, in word or deed, do everything in the name of the Lord Jesus, giving thanks to God the Father through him (3:17).

Christ Connection:
Jesus possesses the fullness of God, and it is through him all things were created.

Application:
Colossians teaches us to stay Christ-focused in our pursuit of holiness. We never mature past the gospel; we mature in the gospel. As believers, we must know the truth and guard against empty deceit and false teaching. At the same time, we must not disconnect knowing truth from holy living. As we are immersed in the truth, we need to put off remaining sin and put on the new self that is being renewed after the image of Jesus. Strive for intentional holiness as well as growth in the truth. Furthermore, we need to be mindful of our testimony to outsiders. Our conduct as Christians speaks loudly to those who do not know Christ.

1 THESSALONIANS

Author:
Paul wrote the letter to the Thessalonians

Date:
Paul wrote sometime in the early 50's.

Theme:
First Thessalonians focuses on encouraging new believers and assuring them of the eternal state of those who have died in Christ.

Summary:
First Thessalonians is a warm and encouraging letter. Paul writes to affirm and strengthen the faith of the new believers. The personal nature of Paul's writing communicates his affection for them. While Paul affirms their faith, he urges them to continue steadfastly in holy living. He emphasizes God's will for their lives, which is continued conformity to the likeness of Jesus. The letter also clarifies what happens to a believer when they die. Death is not the end, but those who have died will be raised on the coming Day of the Lord. This is a comforting truth to the Thessalonians who believed their loved ones who died in faith were going to miss the return of Jesus. Paul's final instructions deal with treating church leaders well and godly living in the present age.

Key Passages:
Our gospel came to you not only in word, but also in power and in the Holy Spirit and with full conviction (1:5)

For you know what instructions we gave you through the Lord Jesus. For this is the will of God, your sanctification (4:2-3).

And we urge you, brothers, admonish the idle, encourage the fainthearted, help the weak, be patient with them all (4:14).

Rejoice always, pray without ceasing, give thanks in all circumstances; for this is the will of God in Christ Jesus for you (4:16-18).

Christ Connection:
Jesus is the savior coming again to rescue his people and bring them to where he is.

Application:
1 Thessalonians is a warm example of Christian encouragement and affection for other believers. Paul shows us how to speak to one another as we journey together in the Christian life. When faced with the question of God's will for your life, the answer is your conformity to Jesus. Practically, God's will is personal sanctification manifest in seeking to do good to everyone, rejoicing always, praying without ceasing, and giving thanks in all circumstances. But we must remember that this is a result of the gospel that changes our lives. We can rejoice always, pray often, and give thanks in all situations because Jesus has paid our debt, the Spirit has given us new life, and the Father is pleased to call us sons and daughters.

2 THESSALONIANS

Author:
Paul wrote the 2nd letter to the Thessalonians.

Date:
Second Thessalonians was written shortly after the first letter in the early 50's.

Theme:
Second Thessalonians focuses on end times confusion and how to live in light of Christ's return.

Summary:
The Thessalonians struggled to grasp how the end of time was to play out. Paul writes to comfort them and assure them that they did not miss the return of Jesus. A "man of lawlessness" will arise and claim to be God, and the teaching will lead many astray. Jesus will return and execute vengeance upon those who afflicted his people. The other issue for the Thessalonians was that some were living in idleness and becoming a burden on the church. Some of their views on end times caused many to stop working and idly let the days pass. He tells the Thessalonians to avoid lazy Christians who refuse to work. Working hard is a sign of godliness; if one does not work, one should not eat. Paul concludes by exhorting the Thessalonians to obey his letter and avoid those who don't.

Key Passages:
To this end we always pray for you, that our God may make you worthy of his calling and may fulfill every resolve for good and every work of faith by his power (1:11).

Now may our Lord Jesus Christ himself, and God our Father, who loved us and gave us eternal comfort and good hope through grace, comfort your hearts and establish them in every good work and word (3:16-17).

But the Lord is faithful. He will establish you and guard you against the evil one (3:3).

If anyone is not willing to work, let him not eat (3:10).

Christ Connection:
Jesus is the coming conqueror who will execute divine justice upon the ungodly.

Application:
Second Thessalonians shows that a day of judgment awaits all the ungodly. We might see the ungodly prosper and Christians afflicted, but Jesus will return and make things right. We should not fear or speculate about the end of time; rather, we should live ready. As wickedness increases and ungodliness is celebrated, we must stand firm, proclaim truth, and trust the Lord's protection. As Christians, we are also called to work hard. Laziness has no place in the Christian life. Let us labor diligently and trust God faithfully as we await the return of our Lord and Savior, Jesus Christ.

1 TIMOTHY

Author:
Paul wrote the letter to Timothy, his disciple.

Date:
First Timothy was written toward the end of Paul's life in the early to mid-60s.

Theme:
Paul instructs Timothy on how to lead the church well in leadership, worship, and correcting false teaching.

Summary:
Timothy is a young minister entrusted with the charge to lead well in Ephesus. Paul reminds him of the centrality of the gospel for Christian ministry and how Timothy needs to order the church. Faithful local church ministry combats false teaching and is marked by praying men. Paul instructs Timothy on the qualifications for leaders in the church and how those in the household of faith must behave. The reality that some will depart from the faith should not distract Timothy, but he is to continue to strive and labor because of his hope set on the living God. As Paul concludes his letter, he gives general instructions on what to do with widows, how to discipline an elder, and how to persevere in the faith.

Key Passages:
The aim of our charge is love that issues from a pure heart and a good conscience and a sincere faith (1:5).

For there is one God, and there is one mediator between God and men, the man Christ Jesus (2:5).

Let no one despise you for your youth, but set the believers an example in speech, in conduct, in love, in faith, in purity (4:12).

Fight the good fight of the faith. Take hold of the eternal life to which you were called and about which you made the good confession in the presence of many witnesses (6:12).

Christ Connection:
Jesus is the only mediator between God and man who unites the church to himself.

Application:
First Timothy is a manual for how to do church right. Regardless of the time, society, or cultural context, the principles of how to lead and organize a church remain the same. We are not left to our imagination or devices to create and structure the church or its worship. Praise God. He has given us a manual on how he desires his church to be operated. While we all have preferences in the church, we must understand that anything we do needs to be explicitly or implicitly rooted in God's word. Also, remember that the purpose of the church is the glory of Jesus and the good of his people. We love and labor because our hope is set upon the living God.

2 TIMOTHY

Author:
Paul wrote the 2nd letter to Timothy.

Date:
Second Timothy was written sometime around 67-68 AD.

Theme:
Second Timothy is a call to boldness, endurance, and faithfulness amid difficult times.

Summary:
Second Timothy is Paul's last letter before his execution for the faith. He charges Timothy to demonstrate boldness by reminding him of his calling. As a faithful disciple of Jesus Christ, Timothy must take the word he has received and entrust it to faithful men who can teach others. Paul establishes the unbroken chain of discipleship that must continue till Jesus returns. As Timothy is to teach and instruct, he must be mindful of those who appear godly but practice all manners of wickedness. He must rest upon the authority and sufficiency of Scripture as he preaches the word in and out of season. Paul's final appeal is to see Timothy one last time before his execution.

Key Passages:
For God gave us a spirit not of fear but of power and love and self-control (1:7).

And what you have heard from me in the presence of many witnesses entrust to faithful men who will be able to teach others also (2:2).

All Scripture is breathed out by God and profitable for teaching, for reproof, for correction, and for training in righteousness, that the man of God may be complete, equipped for every good work (3:16-17).

Preach the word; be ready in season and out of season, reprove, rebuke and exhort, with complete patience and teaching (4:2).

Christ Connection:
Jesus is the giver of life, immortality, hope, and comfort for every believer as they approach the end of life on earth.

Application:
If 1 Timothy is a manual for doing church well, then 2 Timothy is a manual for doing discipleship well. We must be reminded and encouraged to be bold, faithful, and finish well. As one faithful generation passes on to glory, the successive one rises and takes the baton. Everyone who is a follower of Jesus Christ is a part of the unbroken chain of discipleship. As faithful disciples, we must trust in the power of God's word to convict and conform God's people for his glory. The Lord calls us to be faithful in the sharing of his word. The call to faithfulness is not for the faint of heart, but it is rewarding. Paul reminds us of the importance of finishing well in this life. May our motto be "he/she finished well." Until that day, continue to fight the good fight of faith and lay hold of the eternal life to which you have been called.

TITUS

Author:
Paul wrote the letter to Titus.

Date:
Paul wrote sometime in the 60's.

Theme:
Titus is filled with instructions on how to order church, family, and life in the community.

Summary:
Titus is a short letter that combines and summarizes much of the material found in 1 & 2 Timothy. Paul outlines the requirements for elders and the danger of some locals on the island of Crete. In a healthy church, doctrine and practice must align. Older saints serve as examples to the younger. Multigenerational relationships strengthen the church community and perpetuate the chain of discipleship. Christians are to behave as examples even toward outsiders in speech and conduct, knowing they represent Jesus. Paul's final instruction deals with expelling divisive people from the church. Every command and instruction is rooted in the gospel; Titus could be summarized as a picture of a gospel-centered church.

Key Passages:
In hope of eternal life, which God, who never lies, promised before the ages began (1:2).

Show yourself in all respects to be a model of good works, and in your teaching show integrity, dignity, and sound speech that cannot be condemned, so that an opponent may be put to shame, having nothing evil to say about us (2:7-8).

He saved us, not because of works done by us in righteousness, but according to his own mercy, by the washing of regeneration and renewal of the Holy Spirit (3:5).

As for a person who stirs up division, after warning him once and then twice, have nothing more to do with him, knowing such a person is warped and sinful; he is self-condemned (3:10-11).

Christ Connection:
Jesus gave himself to redeem his people from a wicked life and is, therefore, the enabler and motivator of Christian behavior.

Application:
Our behavior and conduct come as a result of the gospel. The gospel-centered church acts according to the instructions in Titus because of the transforming grace of God manifested in the life, death, and resurrection of Jesus. Legalism places good works before the gospel, not an error but a false religion. When we struggle and feel like we are just going through the motions in the Christian life, we need to be reminded of the gospel that saves, transforms, and enables us to live in a manner worthy of our calling. Healthy churches are made up of healthy Christians who have healthy practices. Be part of the body life in the church and contribute to a culture of grace and good works.

PHILEMON

Author:
Paul wrote the short letter to his friend Philemon.

Date:
Paul wrote while in prison in Rome around 60 AD.

Theme:
Philemon focuses on restoring relationships between fellow believers in Jesus Christ.

Summary:
Philemon had a slave named Onesimus who stole from him and ran away. In his escape, Onesimus encountered Paul in Rome and converted to Christianity. Paul writes to his friend Philemon, a fellow believer, to welcome Onesimus back as more than a slave. Paul's appeal for reconciliation comes from the shared love among followers of Jesus Christ. Onesimus is sent back to Philemon and is even the one who carries the letter to his master. Paul demonstrates the gospel in his willingness to pay the debt incurred by Onesimus. After his imprisonment, Paul plans to visit his brother Philemon and looks forward to enjoying fellowship together. He gives confidence that Philemon and Onesimus will do the right thing because of the gospel.

Key Passages:
I thank my God always when I remember you in my prayers, because I hear of your love and of the faith that you have toward the Lord Jesus and for all the saints (4-5).

I appeal to you for my child, Onesimus, whose father I became in my imprisonment (10).

For this perhaps is why he was parted from you for a while, that you might have him back forever, no longer as a bondservant but more than a bondservant, as a beloved brother (15-16).

If he has wronged you at all, or owes you anything, charge that to my account (18).

Christ Connection:
Jesus' reconciliation of sinful humans to a holy God is how reconciliation between believers is possible.

Application:
Christians forgive. No matter the wrong done to us, we can forgive and reconcile with others. Although Onesimus was wrong, he demonstrated true repentance when he returned to Philemon. When we sin against another, we must be willing to do the right thing even if it hurts or costs us. Christians who refuse reconciliation deny in practice the gospel they claim to trust. Christians are to forgive and love without expecting something in return, celebrate repentance, and praise restoration. We are reconciled to God through the death of Christ, and as a result, we can be reconciled with one another for Jesus' sake. The gospel witness is ruined by grudges, holding offenses, and bitterness. All these created disunity and hurt the one holding on to them the most. We are free to forgive, love, and live.

JONATHAN SOLE

THE GENERAL LETTERS

HEBREWS

Author:
The author of Hebrews is anonymous.

Date:
The letter was written sometime in the middle of the first century.

Theme:
Hebrews focuses on the supremacy of Jesus and calls the recipients to persevere in faith.

Summary:
The author makes three significant points: Jesus is greater than the angels, Moses, and the Levitical priesthood. The Hebrews faced trials and needed encouragement to continue steadfastly in the faith. They are warned of the danger of falling away and reverting to mere Judaism. Jesus is the final high priest and the mediator of a new and better covenant. The old (Mosaic) covenant has been fulfilled in Christ as he sacrificed himself for sinners. The proper response is faith and trust in Jesus Christ for cleansing sins and reconciliation with God the Father. Faith has always been the means through which salvation is realized. The author uses the saints of the O.T. as an example of faith. The letter closes with final instructions for how to live a faithful life for the glory of Jesus.

Key Passages:
He is the radiance of the glory of God and the exact imprint of his nature, and he upholds the universe by the word of his power. After making purification for sins, he sat down at the

right hand of the Majesty on high (1:3).

For the word of God is living and active, sharper than any two-edged sword, piercing to the division of soul and of spirit, of joints and of marrow, and discerning the thoughts and intentions of the heart (2:12).

Now faith is the assurance of things hoped for, the conviction of things not seen (11:1)

Strive for peace with everyone, and for the holiness without which no one will see the Lord (12:14).

Christ Connection:
Jesus is the great high priest who offered himself as a sacrifice for the sins of his people and implemented the new covenant.

Application:
Hebrews shows Christ's supremacy over all things and the sufficiency of Christ for our salvation. When we have doubts or are pressured to give up, we are to gaze upon Jesus Christ. His accomplishments are our credentials to enter eternal life. Our assurance and confidence rests upon what Jesus has done, not what we do. Since we are surrounded by the faithful, we can also pursue faithfulness and holiness as the children of God. We do because Christ has done. Trust him, pursue faithfulness, and glorify God. We lay aside every weight and sin which clings so closely by looking to Jesus, the author and perfector of our faith.

JAMES

Author:
James, the half-brother of Jesus, wrote the letter that bears his name.

Date:
The letter is probably one of the earliest New Testament writings, sometime in the 40s or early 50s.

Theme:
True saving faith will result in Christians showing good works.

Summary:
James writes to a community of believers struggling to understand their new freedom in Christ. In the second chapter he challenges them to make sure they puts action to their faith. Faith without good works is a dead faith. In addition to his charge to put faith to work he also encourages his readers to have the proper perspective on trials. James gives timeless lessons on the power of the tongue, marks of true wisdom, the danger of presumption, and the power of faithful prayer. The short letter has been likened to the Proverbs of the New Testament. He concludes with the encouragement to help one another in the Christian walk.

Key Passages:
Count it all joy, my brothers, when you meet trials of various kinds (1:2).

But be doers of the word, and not hearers only, deceiving

yourselves (1:22).

So also faith by itself, if it does not have works, is dead (2:17).

Therefore, confess your sins to one another and pray for one another, that you may be healed. The prayer of a righteous person has great power as it is working (5:16).

Christ Connection:
Jesus is the fulfillment of every one of James' exhortations. He suffered well, obeyed perfectly, was impartial in all his dealings, and is the wisdom of the Father incarnate.

Application:
James is practical and hits us where it hurts on many levels. If we are honest, we can count trials as everything but joy. We must fight to remain impartial, and our tongues get us in trouble more often than we care to admit. While James exhorts us, we recognize it is for our good. We will miss the point of the letter if our takeaway is to try harder. Beloved, we must rest in the reality that Jesus fulfilled every exhortation in James, and he, by his grace and through the Spirit, has enabled us to obey the commands of his word. Only those who are saved by grace through faith can faithfully live out the truth given in this letter. James needs clarification for many think his statement of the relationship between faith and works contradicts Paul. James means that true faith equals salvation, which results in good works. He compliments Paul in Ephesians.

1 PETER

Author:
Peter, the apostle of Jesus Christ, is the author.

Date:
Peter writes some time shortly before his martyrdom in the mid-60s.

Theme:
Peter writes to instruct believers how to suffer well as theyare being marginalized by society.

Summary:
As the Christian community is becoming distinct from Judaism, they are recognized as acting ethically different. They were not being outright physically persecuted for their faith, but they were being maligned and marginalized because of their commitment to purity. Peter combats this discouraging reality by reminding them of their hope and status as sojourners and exiles on the road to glory. As a result, believers are to be submissive to authority, model the God-given design of marriage, and commit to doing good while suffering. Suffering as a Christian is to be expected, and believers are no more like Jesus than when they suffer for him and with him. Peter exhorts elders to care for the flock of God and the rest of the community to live humbly while resisting evil.

Key Passages:
Though you have not seen him, you love him. Though you do not now see him, you believe in him and rejoice with joy that is inexpressible and filled with glory (1:8).

Beloved, I urge you as sojourners and exiles to abstain from the passions of the flesh which wage war against your soul (2:11).

But in your hearts honor Christ the Lord as holy, always being prepared to make a defense to anyone who asks you for a reason for the hope that is in you; yet do it with gentleness and respect (3:15).

Therefore let those who suffer according to God's will entrust their souls to a faithful Creator while doing good (4:19).

Christ Connection:
Jesus is the chief Shepherd who suffered well, leaving his people an example to follow.

Application:
All Scripture is relevant and profitable, yet 1 Peter is a book for this time. Across the globe, Christianity is increasingly marginalized, especially in the post-Christian West. Peter sets us straight on thinking about our residence as sojourners and exiles. Peter's letter teaches us how to live faithfully and suffer well. We are most valuable to this life when we live for the future. In suffering, look beyond the immediate to the eternal, for Christ also suffered, the righteous for the unrighteous, to bring us to God. Live well, suffer well, and finish well to the glory of God.

2 PETER

Author:
Simon Peter identifies himself as the letter's author, who bears his name.

Date:
Peter likely wrote this letter shortly before he died in 67 or 68 AD.

Theme:
2 Peter combats heresy and calls believers to diligence as they await the return of Jesus.

Summary:
2 Peter warns that false teachers will arise among the Christian faith. True believers must beware and recognize false teaching because the actions and attitudes accompanying it are usually greed, sensuality, and untrue words. Peter wants his readers to know the truth; he was an eyewitness to the truth as he stood on the mount and saw Jesus transfixed in all his glory. Another sign of false teachers is that they scoff at the idea of a second coming of Jesus. Peter lets it be known that just as God destroyed the earth with water, he will one day destroy it with fire at the return of Jesus. Judgment is a reality, so the faithful must remain diligent and continue to grow in the grace and knowledge of the Lord Jesus Christ.

Key Passages:
Therefore, brothers, be all the more diligent to confirm your calling and election, for if you practice these qualities you will never fall (1:10).

For no prophecy was ever produced by the will of man, but men spoke from God as they were carried along by the Holy Spirit (1:21).

The Lord is not slow to fulfill his promise as some count slowness, but is patient toward you, not wishing that any should perish, but that all should reach repentance (3:9).

But grow in the grace and knowledge of our Lord and Savior Jesus Christ. To him be the glory both now and to the day of eternity. Amen (3:18).

Christ Connection:
The prophetic words of Scripture find their fulfillment in Jesus, the beloved Son of God.

Application:
Not all people who use the Christian vocabulary or claim to be a teacher of the faith are genuine. As believers, we must discern the actions and attitudes of self-proclaimed religious leaders. To tell the truth from error, we must know God's word and Son and experience God's grace. Anything that does not draw us closer to Jesus in affection and conformity is not from God. Also, be encouraged; Jesus is returning, and when he does, we will be with him for all eternity. Until that day, continue to remain diligent and commit to growing in the grace and knowledge of the Lord Jesus.

1 JOHN

Author:
The apostle John, who wrote the gospel of John, authored the letter that bears his name.

Date:
The date is not conclusive, but it was probably written sometime near the end of the first century.

Theme:
John writes to give true believers assurance of salvation and the hope of eternal life.

Summary:
John, like Peter, combats a first-century heresy. Some were claiming to have a better form of knowledge, and they denied Jesus came in the flesh. Furthermore, they claimed they were without sin, thus diminishing the significance of the bloody death of Jesus on the cross. The believing community was rattled by this teaching and began to wonder if they were the ones who believed a false doctrine. John's letter reassurances them that those who confess Jesus, continue in the faith, and demonstrate self-sacrificing love are the ones born of God. John concludes his letter by telling his readers that he writes that so they may know they have eternal life.

Key Passages:
If we confess our sins, he is faithful and just to forgive us our sin and to cleanse us from all unrighteousness (1:9).

Do not love the world or the things in the world. If anyone loves the world, the love of the Father is not in him (2:15).

By this we know love, that he laid down his life for us, and we ought to lay down our lives for the brothers (3:16).

There is no fear in love, but perfect love casts our fear. For fear has to do with punishment, and whoever fears has not been perfected in love (4:18).

Christ Connection:
Jesus appeases the wrath of the Father and stands as the advocate for all who have faith in him.

Application:
Doubt and lack of assurance hit every believer at one point or another. We must understand the difference between assurance and security. Our security is objective and accomplished in Christ. Our assurance can ebb and flow in this life. When we reach a crisis of faith, 1 John is our go-to book. Some of his assurance tests will challenge us and lead to repentance and restoration. The promises of his letter are for us to claim as we seek to live faithfully, even with the remaining sin in us. Believer, when you sin, make it a practice to run to Jesus, who delights in forgiveness, serves as your advocate, and has exhausted God's wrath against your sin. He is faithful to forgive and cleanse. If God forgives our sins, we need to forgive our sins. Do not carry the guilt that God has graciously discharged through his Son. God has loving made you his child in whom he delights.

2 JOHN

Author:
The apostle John has traditionally been recognized as the author.

Date:
The short letter was likely written sometime near the end of the first century.

Theme:
Beware of some preachers who speak the name of Jesus but carry a false message.

Summary:
2 John could be considered the summary of 1 John. Similar themes surface, such as the commandment to love, reject false teaching, and complete joy. The elect lady John addresses is probably a code name for a specific congregation. The children of the elect sister at the end of his letter are likely another congregation. John makes the connection that true believers not only know the truth but live the truth. John, the apostle of love, never separates truth and love but demonstrates their compatibility. Christians, out of love for Christ and each other, must shun false teachers, for greeting them is the same as joining them.

Key Passages:
The elder to the elect lady and her children, who I love in truth, and not only I, but also all who know the truth (1).

And this is love, that we walk according to his commandments;

this is the commandment, just as you have heard from the beginning, so that you should walk in it (6).

Everyone who goes ahead and does not abide in the teaching of Christ, does not have God. Whoever abides in the teaching has both the Father and the Son (9).

The children of your elect sister greet you (13).

Christ Connection:
Jesus is the true Son of God who came and took upon himself human flesh.

Application:
Although this letter is short, it is packed with truth. False teachers arise in every generation. As followers of Jesus, we must know the truth to avoid false teachers. While we might not welcome them into our homes, we can put their books on our shelves or watch them on our screens. John warns us that a love for Jesus and the gospel compels us to reject those who pervert the message. Let us be careful of who we listen to and who we would recommend to others. Jesus has given us good pastors and teachers to help guide us, warn us, and disciple us in the truth. Furthermore, avoid falling into the danger of separating truth from love. They go hand in hand, and John demonstrates how one complements the other. Our zeal for truth grows as we walk in transparent love for one another. May we give thanks for John's timely instruction.

3 JOHN

Author:
The apostle John wrote 3 John.

Date:
Third John was likely written in the early 90's AD.

Theme:
Third John warns church leaders about those who try to take all authority in the church.

Summary:
John addresses his letter to the beloved Gaius. Gaius is either a faithful church member or possibly an elder in the local church. Gaius represents godly leadership by doing good to strangers who are also brothers in the faith. Gaius welcomes and supports traveling ministers of the gospel. John warns of Diotrephes, who desires position, rejects authority, speaks evil of others, refuses fellowship, and abuses church discipline. John concludes that Diotrephes practices evil and has no relationship with God. Wicked men may creep into the church, but their attitudes and actions will soon manifest.

Key Passages:
I have no greater joy than to hear that my children are walking in the truth (4).

Beloved, it is a faithful thing you do in all your efforts for these brothers, strangers as they are, who testified to your love before the church. You will do well to send them on their journey in a manner worthy of God (5-6).

Diotrephes, who likes to put himself first, does not acknowledge our authority (9).

Beloved, do not imitate evil but imitate good. Whoever does good is from God; whoever does evil has not seen God (11).

Christ Connection:
Jesus is the authority in his church, producing love and submission from his people.

Application:
Beware of Diotrephes. Local churches do not belong to men but are kingdom outposts for Jesus. Diotrephes was not concerned with the mission of God but his power and position. Accountability is necessary for anyone, especially those in local church leadership. Unchecked authority will lead to a culture of abuse, secrecy, and cultish practices. If you are someone in leadership or aspiring to church leadership, ask yourself what motivates you. Gaius serves as a model for good with Diotrephes the bad. John goes as far as to claim that Diotrephes practices evil, and his actions and attitude demonstrate that he does not honestly know God. As church members, we are responsible for what we hear and who we hear it from. Diotrephes warns us against abusive church leadership.

JUDE

Author:
Jude, the younger half-brother of Jesus, wrote the letter.

Date:
Because of the similarities to 2 Peter, Jude dates to around the mid-60s AD.

Theme:
Jude calls upon his readers to contend for the faith, expose false teachings, and persevere.

Summary:
Jude is ready for battle. His charge is to contend for the faith that was once and for all delivered to the saints. False teachers had crept into the church, and they relied on dreams, practiced sensuality, rejected authority, and blaspheme. Jude reminds his recipients of the coming judgment against the ungodly and the victory the Lord will achieve. As a result of these realities, Jude encourages the believers to persevere in faith and love. The believing community was to show mercy to the weak and seek to save others by snatching them out of the fire. Jude concludes with a grand doxology, reminding readers that Jesus will present them blamelessly with great joy.

Key Passages:
I found it necessary to write appealing to you to contend for the faith that was once for all delivered to the saints (3).

"Behold, the Lord comes with ten thousands of his holy ones, to execute judgment on all and to convict all the ungodly of all

their deeds of ungodliness that they have committed" (14-15).

But you, beloved, building yourselves up in your most holy faith and praying in the Holy Spirit, keep yourselves in the love of God, waiting for the mercy of our Lord Jesus Christ that leads to eternal life (20-21).

To the only God, our Savior, through Jesus Christ our Lord, be glory, majesty, dominion, and authority, before all time and now and forever. Amen (25).

Christ Connection:
Jesus is the savior of his people, the judge of the wicked, and hope for the world.

Application:
Our duty as followers of Jesus is to stand firm in the faith. At times, we will contend against false teachers that lead others astray. While the Christian faith is peaceful, it is not passive, and Jude instructs us on the importance of opposing the wicked. Fighting battles is draining, so Jude calls on us to persevere. We continue in the faith by praying in the Spirit, dwelling on God's love, and patiently awaiting the final return of Jesus Christ. While we persevere, we show mercy to the doubters and help protect our brothers and sisters from falling into sin. In other words, be the church. At the end of our time, remember, it is Jesus, with great joy and possibly even a smile on his face, who will present us blameless before the hosts of heaven and glory of his Father. You are his trophy of grace!

REVELATION

Author:
The Apostle John identifies himself as the author of the Revelation.

Date:
Revelation is the last New Testament book written toward the end of the 1st century AD.

Theme:
God wins, and Jesus Christ, the King of Kings, triumphs and brings final salvation to his Bride, the church.

Summary:
The book serves as the fitting bookend of Scripture. Revelation is addressed to seven churches facing a variety of issues. After the context-specific address, John moves into a series of visions ranging from heaven's throne room to the judgment of the wicked. The cosmic battle that has gone on between the Seed of the Woman and the Serpent is depicted in highly symbolic language. The church of Jesus Christ was suffering persecution, and John wrote to comfort them in their trial by pointing toward the triumph of Jesus at the end of the age. The future events of the final four chapters detail the union between Jesus and the church, the ultimate defeat of the Serpent, the final judgment, and the completion of the kingdom of God in the new heavens and earth.

Key Passages:
To him who loves us and has freed us from our sins by his blood and made us a kingdom, priests to his God and Father, to him

be glory and dominion forever and ever. Amen (1:5-6).

"Holy, holy, holy, is the Lord God Almighty, who was and is and is to come!" (4:8).

Let us rejoice and exult and give him the glory, for the marriage of the Lamb has come, and his Bride has made herself ready; it was granted her to clothe herself with fine linen, bright and pure" (19:7-8).

"He will wipe away every tear from their eyes, and death shall be no more, neither shall there be mourning, nor crying, nor pain anymore, for the former things have passed away" (21:4).

Christ Connection:
Jesus is the triumphant one who slays the dragon and brings his bride, the church, home.

Application:
Christian, you are victorious because Christ is the victor. We have strength for today and hope for tomorrow because Jesus has and will crush all his enemies. We can live triumphantly today since we know how the story ends. Be encouraged; God wins, the future is set, and the day comes when our dwelling place is with Jesus. Remember, we are more than conquerors through him who loved us; we get to share that love with others as Jesus builds his kingdom for his glory and our good. We will be with our savior and our often weak faith will be replaced with sight. Death and sin will be no more. Perfect obedience, fellowship, and relationships for eternity, Amen!

CONCLUSION

The Seed promised in Genesis reigns as King of Kings and Lord of Lords in Revelation. The rescue of sinners was accomplished by the incarnate Son of God, Jesus Christ. The story begins with God's paradise and his image bearers walking in fellowship with him and concludes with his image bearers dwelling in paradise with him. The King crushes the evil one and rescues his people for eternity. The OT tells the story of Israel and bringing forth this King. The NT tells us of his arrival, redemption, and return. Now, we await Jesus' return and the completion of his kingdom.

I hope this book was helpful to you in grasping the big picture of the 66 books of the Bible. I pray you have been strengthened in your faith, grown more profound in your understanding, and abounding more in your love for your Savior, his word, and his church. Books about the Bible can change our minds, but the books of the Bible can change our hearts. May our hearts be ever-changing as we behold the glory of God in the face of Jesus Christ through the Holy Spirit-inspired Word.

Many have said that the Bible is the only book that reads you as you read it. As you approach the word of God, do so humbly, honestly, and willingly. Our posture must be to let the word of God conform and reform our thinking, theology, practice, and devotion. For the end of all things is the glory of God manifest in his Son and in our lives of faithfulness and obedience toward him as revealed in his Word.